Filtered
through
Love

THE SOVEREIGNTY OF
GOD IN ACTION

ROWLAND BUGDEN

Ordering Information:

BookTrail Agency
8838 Sleepy Hollow Rd.
Kansas City, MO 64114

Printed in the United States of America

CONTENTS

INTRODUCTION

Suggested Background Reading: Psalm 139

Hallelujah! For the Lord our God the Almighty reigns.
—Revelation 19:6

T he Lord our God does, indeed, reign. He is, indeed, Almighty.
It is good to know that He is not a despotic tyrant, treating us as robots, but He leads us and guides us through His great love for us. We may not understand His plans or see the reasons for events that take place around us, but we can rest assured that His ways are best.

Filtered through Love is the result of a series of studies which were prepared for a conference for pastors held in the Philippines in November 2018. The conference title, "The Sovereignty of God in Doctrine and in the Believer's Experience", was chosen by the Filipino organisers.

The early chapters of *Filtered through Love* focus mainly on global issues and think mainly of how the sovereignty of God has an impact on life on an international scale. The middle chapters concentrate more on God's dealings at a national level, largely being concerned with the Jewish people. God promised to raise His Messiah from within the nation of Israel, so we need to see how He kept the Israelites and guided them until His covenant promises had been fulfilled (and beyond). We then look to see how God deals with families and individuals, and how He provides for them and works out His purposes through them.

All aspects of the sovereignty of God apply in all situations, as can be seen throughout scripture. The passages chosen in *Filtered through Love* are just examples to help us look more closely at the way our sovereign God interacts with His creation, how He relates to us, and how we should relate to Him.

Suggested background readings for each chapter have been given, and some questions have also been included to help us consider the applications of God's sovereignty to our lives. These could be useful for group discussion.

The fact that this study exists is, in itself, a testament to the sovereignty of God. In 2017 a pastor from the Philippines sent an email to the church where I serve in Rattlesden, Suffolk, to invite a speaker to this conference. Why he chose Rattlesden, I don't know. He may have tried many other churches before contacting us, or we may have been his first choice, but either way I understand that he was looking for a church with a basis of faith which he felt comfortable with.

Our administrator would not normally take too much notice of an email like that, but she passed it on to me so she could feel that she had not dismissed it out of hand. She expected me to delete it, not wanting to take the responsibility herself for doing so.

I felt the Lord telling me to respond to the pastor, which I did somewhat cautiously. It was soon clear that I had to take this responsibility seriously. I did not know at the time why I was doing something very unusual for me, but I copied the emails to my computer and tucked them into the corner of a memory disc.

All went well until I had a major problem with my email account. The whole account disappeared from my computer, and I was unable to send or receive emails. All those I had received were lost, along with my email address book. I tried to reopen the account, but the system told me that I could not use that email address—it had already been used. I had to start again with a new address, but this did not give me access to my address book or any past emails.

I was now in a difficult situation. I could not receive emails from the Philippine pastor, and I could not send one to him to tell him of my new address or that I was not receiving his emails.

I looked at the emails I had copied, but I did not see any contact details. Time was passing; I was becoming increasingly concerned that I would not be able to make contact.

There was only one thing to do—*pray!*

My prayer was that God would confirm that I was doing the right thing by planning to go to the conference by leading me towards a way of contacting the Filipino pastor and by my ensuring my wife would be happy for me to go!

My wife did agree to give me her blessing to go, but she felt that she would not accompany me. Then I felt God was nudging me to look again at the emails I had copied. When I did so, all seemed as before, until suddenly I noticed that there was a second page to one of the emails. My reply to the pastor's initial invitation was all on one page. I had not noticed that there was a page 2, which proved to be a second copy of the invitation with something extra at the bottom— the pastor's email address. I was able to make contact again, and now I felt sure that God was guiding me by His sovereign will.

THE SOVEREIGNTY OF GOD IN REALITY

Suggested Background Reading: Job 1, 2, 42

We start by looking at the sovereignty of God on a global scale, but it may seem as if the focus is on one man: Job. The purpose of starting with Job is actually to see how God, in His dealings with Job, was exercising His power over Satan.

We first consider the omnipotence of God by thinking about what the word means. It simply tells us that God is all-powerful, but we need to see what that means and how it works out in our daily lives today.

God's omnipotence means that God is able to implement all His holy will. The word *omnipotence*, which means "all-powerful", is made up of two Latin words: *omni*, which means "all", and *potens*, which means "powerful". We can also talk about God's freedom, referring to the fact that His decisions are not limited by any external conditions. God's omnipotence tells us of His own power to do what He decides to do.

This power is frequently mentioned in scripture. For example, the psalmist David calls God "the Lord, mighty in battle!"

> Who is this King of glory?
> The Lord, strong and mighty,
> the Lord, mighty in battle! (Psalm 24:8)

God asked Abraham, "Is anything too hard for the Lord?" (Genesis 18:14).

And He asked Jeremiah the same question. "Behold, I am the Lord, the God of all flesh. Is anything too hard for me?" (Jeremiah 32:27).

Jeremiah certainly understood that this question implies (in the context in which it occurs) that nothing is too hard for the Lord. In fact, he said to God, "Nothing is too hard for you" (Jeremiah 32:17).

The angel Gabriel had a similar message for Mary when announcing the coming of Jesus: "For nothing will be impossible with God" (Luke 1:37).

Jesus told His disciples the same thing: "But with God all things are possible" (Matthew 19:26).

Paul wrote to the church at Ephesus and told them of the power of God, reminding them that His power works within us. "Now to him who is able to do far more abundantly than all that we ask or think, according to the power at work within us" (Ephesians 3:20).

Paul also wrote to the Corinthian church, expressing our relationship with God: "And I will be a father to you, and you shall be sons and daughters to me, says the Lord Almighty" (2 Corinthians 6:18).

The term *Almighty* used by Paul is also found in God's description of Himself in Revelation 1:8: "'I am the Alpha and the Omega,' says the Lord God, 'who is and who was and who is to come, the Almighty.'"

The term *Almighty* (Greek: *Pantokratōr*) suggests the possession of all power and authority.

The psalmist wrote of God's omnipotence in Psalm 115:3: "Our God is in the heavens; he does all that he pleases."

There are other scriptures indicating that God's power is infinite and that He is able to act far beyond what He actually does. For example, God kept the descendants of Abraham alive, even though they had made a golden calf while waiting for Moses to come down from Sinai with the Law. He could have destroyed them and replaced them with a great nation from the offspring of Moses or, as John the Baptist told the Pharisees and Sadducees, with stones. He chose not to do so.

Exodus 32:10 says, "Now therefore let me alone, that my wrath may burn hot against them and I may consume them, in order that I may make a great nation of you."

Matthew 3:9 says, "God is able from these stones to raise up children for Abraham."

However, we must remember that there are some things that God cannot do. God can do whatever is in His will, but His will cannot include anything that would deny His own character. This is why the definition of *omnipotence* is stated in terms of God's ability to do "all His holy will"—and His will is always consistent with His character.

For example, God cannot lie. In Titus 1:2, He is called (literally) "the unlying God" or the "God who never lies". The author of Hebrews says in Hebrews 6:18 that in God's oath and promise, "it is impossible for God to lie." Second Timothy 2:13 says of Christ, "He cannot deny Himself." Furthermore, James 1:13 says, "God cannot be tempted with evil and He Himself tempts no one." Thus, God cannot lie, sin, or act in any way inconsistent with any of His attributes.

This means that it is not entirely accurate to say that God can do anything. Even the foregoing scriptures that use phrases similar to that must be understood within their context to mean that God can do anything He wills to do or anything that is consistent with His character. Although God's power is infinite, His use of that power is qualified by His other attributes, including love, (just as all God's attributes qualify all His actions). So it is important to look at all the attributes of God together and not take any of them in isolation.

God's exercise of power over His creation is also called God's sovereignty. God's sovereignty is His exercise of rule (as "sovereign" or "king") over His creation. This is also linked to God's *providence*.

It is appropriate to realise that God has made us in such a way that we show in our lives some faint reflection of each of His attributes. God has made us creatures with a *will*. We exercise choice and make real decisions regarding the events in our lives. Although our will is not absolutely free in the way God's is, God has nonetheless given us *relative freedom* within our spheres of activity in the universe He has created.

In fact, we feel that we have the ability to exercise our wills and make choices and to do so in a relatively free way. This is a topic we will consider in detail later. This ability to make choices is one of the most significant signs that God made us in His own image. Of course, our desire to exercise our wills and our desire to be free from restraint show that our sinful ways have separated us from God and spoiled His creation. People can become proud and may want a kind of freedom that involves rebellion against God's authority instead of obeying His will.

Nevertheless, when we use our will and our freedom to make choices that are pleasing to God, then we reflect His character and bring glory to Him. When our ability to make free choices is limited by evil governments or by other circumstances, an important part of our godlikeness is suppressed. It is not surprising that we will pay almost any price to maintain our freedom. The American revolutionary Patrick Henry was heard to cry, "Give me liberty or give me death!" This resonates deep within every soul created in the image of God.

We do not, of course, have infinite power or omnipotence any more than we have any of God's other attributes to an infinite degree. But even though we do not have omnipotence, God has given us *power* to bring about results, both physical power and other kinds of power: mental power, spiritual power, persuasive power, and power in various kinds of authority structures, such as family, church, and civil government. In all these areas, the use of power in ways pleasing to God and consistent with His will is again something that brings Him glory as it reflects His own character.

The clearest demonstration in scripture of God's omnipotence comes in the story of Job.

We are introduced to Job as "one who feared God and turned away from evil". We are told in some detail of his wealth and of his concern to be right in God's sight. This resulted in Satan's wanting to pick a quarrel with God and attack Job.

Our first glimpse into heaven shows us the "sons of God" on parade. When Satan appears as well, there is a dialogue between God and Satan. Satan speaks of his activity on earth, which warns us to be aware of the risks we face as God's people. We then read of his challenge to God about Job.

Peter warns us of the activity of Satan on earth in 1 Peter 5:8: "Be sober-minded; be watchful. Your adversary the devil prowls around like a roaring lion, seeking someone to devour."

It is good for us to see this in the light of the omnipotence of God since Peter goes on to encourage his readers to resist Satan, *keeping our faith in God firm*. Peter also goes on to assure us that we may be allowed to suffer for a while, but God will restore us, confirm us, and strengthen us after a limited time.

> Resist him, firm in your faith, knowing that the same kinds
> of suffering are being experienced by your brotherhood

throughout the world. And after you have suffered for a little while, the God of all grace, who has called you to his eternal glory in Christ, will himself restore, confirm, strengthen, and establish you. (1 Peter 5:9–10)

Job certainly experienced that.

Before going any further, let me make it abundantly clear that God never tempts us. He may see fit to test us, as He did Abraham (Genesis 22), and He does allow us to be tempted. James wants us to see testing in a positive light but warns us not to blame God for any temptation to do evil.

Count it all joy, my brothers, when you meet trials of various kinds, for you know that the testing of your faith produces steadfastness. And let steadfastness have its full effect, that you may be perfect and complete, lacking in nothing. … Blessed is the man who remains steadfast under trial, for when he has stood the test, he will receive the crown of life, which God has promised to those who love him. *Let no one say when he is tempted, "I am being tempted by God," for God cannot be tempted with evil, and he himself tempts no one.* But each person is tempted when he is lured and enticed by his own desire. Then desire when it has conceived gives birth to sin, and sin when it is fully grown brings forth death. (James 1:2–4, 12–15; emphasis mine)

Paul also reminds the Corinthian Christians that God is in control, even of our temptation, for, although He does not initiate it, He does restrict it and graciously provide a way of escape. Paul starts by saying that, whatever the temptation, we are not unique in experiencing it.

No temptation has overtaken you that is not common to man. God is faithful, and *he will not let you be tempted beyond your ability*, but with the temptation He will also provide the way of escape, that you may be able to endure it. (1 Corinthians 10:13; emphasis mine)

We also see here that temptation may be direct or indirect. When Jesus was tempted in the wilderness, the temptation was direct.

> Then Jesus was led up by the Spirit into the wilderness to be tempted by the devil. And after fasting forty days and forty nights, he was hungry. And the tempter came and said to him, "If you are the Son of God, command these stones to become loaves of bread." (Matthew 4:1–3)

In the case of Job, the temptation was indirect. It was never suggested to him that he curse God; rather, those things which Satan claimed were the reason for Job's loyalty to God were removed in the hope that he would turn against God.

The significance of this to a discussion about the omnipotence of God is that we are told very clearly *that Satan could attack Job only when he had God's permission to do so*, and then only as far as God allowed him to. This is underlined by the fact that the devastation came in two stages. First (Job 1), Satan was permitted to remove Job's family and wealth but not to touch him personally. This was ineffective at leading Job to sin, but Satan was not able to go farther without coming back to God and asking again.

In the second stage (Job 2), Satan was given permission to touch Job's health, but this was also restricted in that Job's life was to be spared.

God's power over Satan is thus clearly demonstrated, but the story goes further. Satan was also limited in the length of time for which he could oppress Job. By the end of the book of Job (Job 42), we read that God had not only ended Satan's onslaught but also restored Job's family and wealth twofold.

This is why Paul could tell the Corinthians that God would not let us "be tempted beyond our ability".

Question 1. *Can you think of a possible reason why God allowed Satan to make Job suffer?*

Whilst it is good to notice that God did not tempt Job, we are left to draw our own conclusions as to why God allowed Satan to. The fact that God asked Satan about Job suggests that God did have a purpose in mind. There are several possibilities as to what that purpose might be.

Firstly, we could read this as God demonstrating his sovereignty to Satan. This may seem unlikely since Satan would have been only too aware of that already, and it would not be in God's nature to let Job endure such suffering in order to "score points" off Satan.

Secondly, we can probably dismiss the idea that God was demonstrating His sovereignty to Job as he (Job) would not have been aware of the conversations taking place between God and Satan.

Thirdly, God may have been wanting Job to understand the strength of his own faith. Not only did Job end up twice as well off as he had started, but also he came out of the period of temptation and affliction knowing that his faith in God had seen him through a very difficult time.

This last point is also in keeping with the incident in Genesis 22 where God tested Abraham.

> After these things God tested Abraham and said to him, "Abraham!" And he said, "Here am I." He said, "Take your son, your only son Isaac, whom you love, and go to the land of Moriah, and offer him there as a burnt offering on one of the mountains of which I shall tell you." (Genesis 22:1–2)

The phrase "After these things" is significant here. Abraham had just shown a lack of faith in telling Abimelech that Sarah was his sister.

(Actually, this was half true—she was his half-sister.) God had restored his faith by giving him Isaac, and now He was testing Abraham to show him that his faith in God was secure.

This should, surely, make an impact on the way we deal with temptation and testing. We have seen that temptation never comes from God, but it is always with His permission. It always has limits which we can cope with—limits in terms of severity and time—and there will always be a way of escape.

James tells us, "Count it all joy, my brothers, when you meet trials of various kinds, for you know that the testing of your faith produces steadfastness." This may be easier said than done, but it should give us great encouragement as we seek to stay close to our Lord.

We should also notice that Job would also have seen the power of prayer. In Job 42:10 we read, "The Lord restored the fortunes of Job, *when he had prayed for his friends*" (emphasis mine). God had already told the friends, "My servant Job shall pray for you, for I will accept his prayer not to deal with you according to your folly" (v. 8). And in the next verse it is confirmed that "the Lord accepted Job's prayer."

Job prayed from a desperate situation, but he prayed for his friends, not himself. He trusted God even in that state and had full assurance that he was in God's hands.

Job 19:25 reads, "For I know that my Redeemer lives, and at the last he will stand upon the earth."

More important than this, Job understood the sovereignty of God.

We read in Job 42:1-2, "Then Job answered the Lord and said: 'I know that you can do all things, and that no purpose of yours can be thwarted.'"

Job's confidence in the sovereignty of God was confirmed for him when God not only restored his fortune but also doubled what he'd previously had.

As we read of God confronting Satan, we might also think of the many occasions when Jesus was faced with demons. One example is well known:

> And when he came to the other side, to the country of the Gadarenes, two demon-possessed men met him, coming out of the tombs, so fierce that no one could pass that way. And behold, they cried out, "What have you to do with us, O Son of God? Have you come here to torment us before the time?" Now a herd of many pigs was feeding at some distance from them. And the demons begged him, saying, "If you cast us out, send us away into the herd of pigs." And he said to them, "Go." So they came out and went into the pigs, and behold, the whole herd rushed down the steep bank into the sea and drowned in the waters. (Matthew 8:28–32)

There are many occasions recorded in scripture where God intervenes in a direct way which demonstrates His sovereignty.

One such occasion would be the story of Jonah. God told him to go to Nineveh and warn the inhabitants of forthcoming punishment for their wickedness. Jonah's reaction was to head in the opposite direction, but God stopped the ship on which Jonah was trying to reach Spain with a great storm, and He had a great fish ready to swallow Jonah.

Another example is in the parting of the Red Sea to allow the Israelites to cross, but stopping the Egyptian army.

Question 2. *Why does God allow **us** to suffer?*

We could also think of Balaam, who was going on a journey against God's instruction.

> Then the angel of the Lord went ahead and stood in a narrow place, where there was no way to turn either to the right or to the left. When the donkey saw the angel of the Lord, she lay down under Balaam. And Balaam's anger was kindled, and he struck the donkey with his staff. Then the Lord opened the mouth of the donkey, and she said to Balaam, "What have I done to you, that you have struck me these three times?" And Balaam said to the donkey, "Because you have made a fool of me. I wish I had a sword in my hand, for then I would kill you." And the donkey said to Balaam, "Am I not your donkey, on which you have ridden all your life long to this day? Is it my habit to treat you this way?" And he said, "No."
>
> Then the Lord opened the eyes of Balaam, and he saw the angel of the Lord standing in the way, with his drawn sword in his hand. And he bowed down and fell on his face. (Numbers 22:26–31)

This is a positive intervention by the sovereign God to stop Balaam from doing the wrong thing for Israel by bringing a curse on them rather than a blessing.

In closing this chapter, let us stop and consider how we should think of God. The most majestic of all of God's names is "the Lord of Hosts".

> For behold, he who forms the mountains and creates the wind, and declares to man what is his thought, who makes the morning darkness, and treads on the heights of the earth—the Lord, the God of hosts, is his name! (Amos 4:13)

The last line of this verse can be put as "YHVH Elohim Sabaoth is His Name."

YHVH is God's personal name.

By pairing YHVH with the Hebrew word *Sabaoth*, we get a title that is often translated as "Lord of Hosts" or "Lord of Armies". But those titles are so limiting in contrast to the true significance of this name.

Sabaoth is the feminine form of the Hebrew word *tsaba*, which means "army", "war", or "warfare". The first time we see the word *tsaba* is in the completion of Creation: "Thus the heavens and the earth were completed, and all their hosts [seba'am]" (Genesis 2:1).

Here and in other scriptures, the masculine form of *tsaba* refers to the entire universe and all of God's perfect creation on earth. He made it. He is Lord over all of it: lightning and wind, sun and moon, man and woman, animals and plants—everything!

Now, imagine the result when we combine *tsaba* with the personal name of God, YHVH—we get a name that gives us a glimpse into how marvellously almighty and all-powerful He truly is.

Let us think of God's majesty through His name and title: YHVH Sabaoth—the Lord, the God of Hosts!

We'll return to this theme in the last chapter of *Filtered through Love*.

> Not to us, O Lord, not to us, but to your name give glory, for the sake of your steadfast love and your faithfulness! Why should the nations say, "Where is their God?" Our God is in the heavens; he does all that he pleases. (Psalm 115:1–3)

Chapter 2

THE SOVEREIGNTY OF GOD IN HISTORY

Suggested Background Reading:

1 Samuel 23, 2 Samuel 22 and Psalm 18

In 1 Samuel 23, we read of David's escape from Saul on several occasions. In 2 Samuel 22 and Psalm 18, we find David's song of praise and thankfulness to God who had protected him from Saul. David was careful to ask God for instructions before going to a place of conflict. God had planned for David to become king, so He gave him victory over the Philistines at Keilah, also warning David of Saul's approach there. Then He distracted Saul at Maon to keep David safe.

The hand of the sovereign God is unmistakeable here, but we need to consider these events in the context of the whole sweep of human history throughout the Old Testament and into the New.

The plans which God made for the human race began to be revealed as far back as the Fall. We read in Genesis 3:14–15, "Because you have done this, cursed are you above all livestock and above all beasts of the field; on your belly you shall go, and dust you shall eat all the days of your life. I will put enmity between you and the woman, and between your offspring and her offspring; he shall bruise your head, and you shall bruise his heel."

This is the earliest sign—spoken to the serpent!—that God is going to use a human to bring about the restoration of a sinless people for Himself. From this point onwards, the Old Testament points towards the coming of Christ as our Saviour and Redeemer. There are very many times in human history when we might wonder how God would have His way, except that we know the answer to this by looking back from our privileged position in the twenty-first century.

The time came when the people on earth were so evil that God was angry and prepared to destroy human life. He could not do this completely, however, since He had already stated that a descendent of Eve would be the Redeemer, so He found a man who, with his family, could be trusted to maintain the human race: Noah.

> And God said to Noah, "I have determined to make an end of all flesh, for the earth is filled with violence through them. Behold, I will destroy them with the earth. Make yourself an ark of gopher wood. Make rooms in the ark, and cover it inside and out with pitch. ... For behold, I will bring a flood of waters upon the earth to destroy all flesh in which is the breath of life under heaven. Everything that is on the earth shall die. But I will establish my covenant with you, and you shall come into the ark, you, your sons, your wife, and your sons' wives with you." (Genesis 6:13–14, 17–18)

Not only does this show that God was keeping His word to the serpent about maintaining the human race, but also it is the first time God speaks of a covenant. Noah was also kept in the presence of God by being told to "come" into the ark.

We are told what covenant was given to Noah when the flood is over and Noah has made burnt offerings to the Lord.

> And when the Lord smelt the pleasing aroma, the Lord said in his heart, "I will never again curse the ground because of man, for the intention of man's heart is evil from his youth. Neither will I ever again strike down every living creature as I have done. While the earth remains, seed-time and harvest, cold and heat, summer and winter, day and night, shall not cease." (Genesis 8:21–22)

We read in Genesis 9:9, "Behold, I establish my covenant with you and your offspring after you."

God had made a covenant with Noah, but He also said that there was another covenant to come. The saving of God's people (Noah and his family) and the destruction of everyone else is a picture of the salvation of God's people (His church) when evil will finally be dealt with.

The greatest revelation of God's sovereign plans in the early Old Testament came when God made His covenant with Abraham (Genesis 15). This was done with all the formalities of a legal bond, and Abraham was left in no doubt as to the sincerity of the occasion. God also did this at a time when Abraham was childless and advanced in years. God specified that it would be his son through which the covenant would be kept.

> Abram said, "O Lord God, what will you give me, for I continue childless, and the heir of my house is Eliezer of Damascus?" And Abram said, "Behold, you have given me no offspring, and a member of my household will be my heir." And behold, the word of the Lord came to him: "This man shall not be your heir; your very own son shall be your heir."

> And He brought him outside and said, "Look towards heaven, and number the stars, if you are able to number them." Then he said to him, "So shall your offspring be."

> And he believed the Lord, and he counted it to him as righteousness. …
>
> On that day the Lord made a covenant with Abram, saying, "To your offspring I give this land, from the river of Egypt to the great river, the river Euphrates." (Genesis 15:2–6, 18)

When Abraham reached the age of ninety-nine and was still childless, God renewed the covenant with him and his descendants. This time there was something that Abraham was told to do as his part in the covenant—he was to circumcise himself and his male descendants as a sign of their allegiance to God.

> I will make you exceedingly fruitful, and I will make you into nations, and kings shall come from you. And I will establish my covenant between me and you and your offspring after you throughout their generations for an everlasting covenant, to be God to you and to your offspring after you. And I will give to you and to your offspring after you the land of your sojournings, all the land of Canaan, for an everlasting possession, and I will be their God. (Genesis 17:6–8)

God demonstrated His sovereignty once more by giving Abraham and Sarah—also in her nineties—a son, Isaac.

God had promised to establish His covenant with Isaac even before he was born. We read in Genesis 17:21, "But I will establish my covenant with Isaac, whom Sarah shall bear to you at this time next year."

We read in Genesis 24 that God intervened in the choice of a wife for Isaac before formally renewing the covenant with him:

> Sojourn in this land, and I will be with you and will bless you, for to you and to your offspring I will give all these lands, and I will establish the oath that I swore to Abraham

16

> your father. I will multiply your offspring as the stars of heaven and will give to your offspring all these lands. And in your offspring all the nations of the earth shall be blessed, *because Abraham obeyed my voice and kept my charge, my commandments, my statutes, and my laws.* (Genesis 26:3–5; emphasis mine)

The next stage in God's plan unfolded when Isaac became the father of twins, Esau and Jacob. Despite Esau's seniority—even if only by a few minutes—it was Jacob whom God intended to use for His purposes. Despite some of his questionable behaviour, Jacob was given a dramatic insight into his place in God's plans as God renewed the covenant with him, too.

> I am the Lord, the God of Abraham your father and the God of Isaac. The land on which you lie I will give to you and to your offspring. Your offspring shall be like the dust of the earth, and you shall spread abroad to the west and to the east and to the north and to the south, and in you and your offspring shall all the families of the earth be blessed. Behold, I am with you and will keep you wherever you go, and will bring you back to this land. For I will not leave you until I have done what I have promised you. (Genesis 28:13–15)

We would do well to note that there were two specific elements to the covenant, as well as the promise of God's enduring presence with His people.

The first specific promise is that God would give the descendants a homeland.

In Genesis 17:8, God said to Abraham, "And I will give to you and to your offspring after you the land of your sojournings, all the land of Canaan, for an everlasting possession, and I will be their God."

In Genesis 26:3, God said to Isaac, "Sojourn in this land, and I will be with you and will bless you, for to you and to your offspring I will give all these lands, and I will establish the oath that I swore to Abraham your father."

In Genesis 28:13–14, God said to Jacob, "The land on which you lie I will give to you and to your offspring. Your offspring shall be like the dust of the earth, and you shall spread abroad to the west and to the east and to the north and to the south."

The second specific promise was that one of the descendants of the family would be a great blessing to all nations—clearly a reference to the coming of Jesus as our Saviour.

In Genesis 22:18, God said to Abraham, "And in your offspring shall all the nations of the earth be blessed, because you have obeyed my voice."

In Genesis 26:4, God said to Isaac, "And in your offspring all the nations of the earth shall be blessed."

In Genesis 28:14, God said to Jacob, "In you and your offspring shall all the families of the earth be blessed."

This, then, is the significance of what God said to Moses from the burning bush:

> "Moses, Moses!" And he said, "Here I am." Then he said, "Do not come near; take your sandals off your feet, for the place on which you are standing is holy ground." And he said, "I am the God of your father, *the God of Abraham, the God of Isaac, and the God of Jacob.*" And Moses hid his face, for he was afraid to look at God. (Exodus 3:4–6; emphasis mine)

God has named Himself here as the God of the three men through whom He had given the covenant; in doing so, He identifies Himself with the promises He made to them. Effectively, He is saying, "Because I am the God of the covenant and have demonstrated my omnipotence— my sovereign power—in establishing that covenant, I am able to use my power through you to bring my people out of Egypt."

This also tells Moses why God wants to bring the Israelites out of Egypt. He was beginning to deliver on His covenant promises by preparing to take His people to the Promised Land. The covenant had stated very clearly where their homeland was to be.

> To your offspring I give this land, from the river of Egypt to the great river, the river Euphrates, the land of the Kenites, the Kenizzites, the Kadmonites, the Hittites, the Perizzites, the Rephaim, the Amorites, the Canaanites, the Girgashites and the Jebusites. (Genesis 15:18–21)

At the time God spoke to Moses, saying, "I am the God of your father, the God of Abraham, the God of Isaac, and the God of Jacob," the Israelites were in slavery in Egypt. Jacob and his family had moved there to avoid famine when Joseph was the controller of the Egyptian food supplies, some four hundred years earlier. The family had grown into a nation of, possibly, two million people and were now in a position to take possession of the promised homeland and to establish themselves as its occupants.

Question 3. *Why did God tell the Israelites to put animal blood on the doorposts for the last plague in Egypt? Surely He knew who His people were.*

The Exodus of the Israelites from the slavery and bondage of Egypt offers us a number of pictures. God did not need His people to go through the procedure of killing a lamb and spreading the blood around the doorway, but He chose to do so to give us the picture of the Lamb of God being sacrificed and His blood shed so that we might be brought out of our slavery to sin. The Israelites were given the Passover feast to remember this event, and Jesus turned that feast around to our communion feast by giving the symbols a new meaning.

> And he took a cup, and when he had given thanks he said, "Take this, and divide it among yourselves. For I tell you that from now on I will not drink of the fruit of the vine until the kingdom of God comes." And he took bread, and when he had given thanks, he broke it and gave it to them, saying, "This is my body, which is given for you. Do this in remembrance of me." And likewise the cup after they had eaten, saying, "This cup that is poured out for you is the new covenant in my blood." (Luke 22:17–20)

This took place while Jesus was celebrating the Passover with His disciples. The first cup mentioned here (v. 17) is part of the Passover feast. Jesus changed its meaning to be a memorial of His blood (v. 20).

History continues as God gives His people a legal framework by which they should live. This would have been in contrast to the Egyptian way of living, and it established moral and ethical standards, along with rules for worshipping God. The wanderings in the wilderness presented various challenges where God demonstrated His love and care for His people and His ability to supply their needs.

Question 4. *Why did God leave His people in slavery in Egypt for 430 years?*

Many of the laws given at this stage have parallel principles in Christian life today, or they picture events in the life and work of Jesus. God gave a further revelation of His sovereign will, whilst not turning His people into robots.

The Israelites were not permitted to intermarry with other nations; this was to keep the bloodline pure. God had promised that the Messiah would be a descendant of Abraham and said that restricting the nation in this way would ensure that Jesus met this criterion. It also directs us, as Christians, to avoid marriage or business contracts with those who do not own Christ as King and who might draw us away from our worship of God.

The sacrifices and offerings required by God were examples of how Christ's death would atone for the sin of God's people throughout history.

The time in the wilderness also included events such as the plague of serpents:

> And the people became impatient on the way. And the people spoke against God and against Moses, "Why have you brought us up out of Egypt to die in the wilderness? For there is no food and no water, and we loathe this worthless food." Then the Lord sent fiery serpents among the people, and they bit the people, so that many people of Israel died. And the people came to Moses and said, "We have sinned, for we have spoken against the Lord and against you. Pray to the Lord, that he take away the serpents from us." So Moses prayed for the people. And the Lord said to Moses, "Make a fiery serpent and set it on a pole, and everyone who is bitten, when he sees it, shall live." So Moses made a bronze serpent and set it on a pole. And if a serpent bit anyone, he would look at the bronze serpent and live. (Numbers 21:4–9)

We should see the symbolism of looking to a serpent on a pole and linking it to Jesus on the cross. Jesus, Himself, makes it clear that this symbolism is intended, including the resulting gift of life: "And as Moses lifted up the serpent in the wilderness, so must the Son of Man be lifted up, that whoever believes in him may have eternal life" (John 3:14–15).

We may also notice that the serpent is a symbol of evil since Satan used one to tempt Eve in the Garden of Eden. The plague of serpents in the wilderness was sent as a punishment for the evil of the Israelites, and the symbolism continues with Jesus identifying Himself with the serpent on the pole as He was "made to be sin" for our sakes.

As we read in 2 Corinthians 5:21, "For our sake he made him to be sin who knew no sin, so that in him we might become the righteousness of God."

As we trace history onward, we see part of the covenant of God being completed as the Israelites enter the Promised Land under God's direction through Joshua. The parallel for us is our entry into heaven with Christ, the only battle involved with that having already been won on the cross.

The remaining part of the covenant—sending the Messiah as a direct descendant of Abraham—was still being awaited.

The period of the judges saw the Israelites caught up in a downward spiral. When God blessed them and all seemed to be going well, they became complacent and drifted away from God. But soon they would drift into idolatry and the worship of pagan gods. As a punishment— or, rather, to bring them back to God—God would send a foreign nation to oppress them. When the people repented and turned back to God, appealing for relief, God would raise up a judge to lead them against the invaders. Life would then become good again, and the people would, once more, become complacent, starting the cycle again.

Repeatedly we are told that God was in supreme control of events with phrases such as this: "The people of Israel did what was evil in the sight of the Lord, and the Lord *gave them into the hand of Midian* for seven years" (Judges 6:1; emphasis mine).

During this time, there are many instances of God working on behalf of His people, using the judges to drive out the invaders. As this period progresses, the need emerges for the Israelites to have a king as their earthly leader, under God's direction. Their ability to look to God for themselves had been eroded by their evil ways.

Saul, the first of the kings, started well, but it was not long before he lost sight of God's leading. God prepared David to succeed him as king, but this made Saul jealous. Saul saw him as a threat so he sought to "remove" him. We have already seen in 2 Samuel 22 and Psalm 18 how David praised God for delivering him from Saul. David clearly understood that it was in the sovereign will of God that Saul's evil intentions towards him had been thwarted.

As we move on to consider David as the second king of the Israelites, we keep one eye on the covenant and notice that David, being from the Tribe of Judah was, indeed, a descendant of Abraham. Also, fitting this in with prophecies regarding the coming Messiah, we see that Jesus would be a "root and branch" descendant of Jesse, David's father. At this point we can take a big jump through history and see how Jesus did, in fact, descend "root and branch" from Jesse.

The prophecy linking Jesus as a descendant of Jesse is found in Isaiah: "There shall come forth a shoot from the stump of Jesse, and a branch from his roots shall bear fruit" (Isaiah 11:1).

Turning to the genealogies of Jesus in the Gospels, we have two accounts of Jesus's ancestry.

Matthew starts his account of the life of Jesus by tracing Him from Abraham (v. 1)—a vital link in order to fulfil the covenant—through Solomon, son of David, son of Jesse (v. 6), another vital link in order to fulfil the covenant. However, on closer inspection, we see that the ancestral line goes to Joseph, husband of Mary, mother of Jesus (v. 16). Matthew was aware that Joseph was not the father of Jesus, but he made the link because the Jews would not have accepted a bloodline to the mother—only men were acceptable for a genealogy. It is quite remarkable that Matthew included the names of some of the mothers at all, but none of them was in the direct bloodline.

Luke also gives us a genealogy of Jesus (chapter 3). He starts with Adam and traces the line to Abraham. From Abraham to David he provides the same list, but he then takes us through a different son of David—Nathan. From here the list is totally different, taking us not to Joseph but to Mary herself. This establishes a complete and unbroken bloodline from Abraham to Jesus.

Both genealogies include the name of the son of Jacob—Judah. This is also important since the Messiah was to be "the Lion of the Tribe of Judah": "Weep no more; behold, the Lion of the tribe of Judah, the Root of David, has conquered, so that he can open the scroll and its seven seals" (Revelation 5:5).

God worked through the history of the Israelites to ensure that His Son was a "branch" of Jesse—through Joseph—and a "shoot" from the stump of Jesse, through Mary.

Not only has God delivered on His covenant, but also He has shown us very clearly that Jesus was that promised Messiah and that the prophecies about Him have been fulfilled in great detail.

The timing of the coming of Jesus is also very important. All the public records were kept in the Temple. The ministry of Jesus was from about AD 25 to AD 28. In about AD 70, the Romans attacked Jerusalem and totally destroyed the Temple. During the life of Jesus, anyone could have checked that He truly fitted the covenant details, and Matthew and Luke would almost certainly have used these records for their Gospels. Had Jesus come any later, these records might not have been available for inspection.

The final completion of the covenant with Abraham came with the greatest events in the history of humankind. When Jesus was born at Bethlehem, the covenant had been fulfilled in a technical sense. The promised Messiah had been given, but the spirit of the covenant was delivered when Jesus proved Himself to be that Messiah by His death and resurrection. These were not only the greatest events in history but are also the greatest display of God's love for His creation and His sovereignty over it.

God used the combined forces of the Israelite hierarchy, with all their blinkered ritualism, and the military might of the Roman occupying power to bring about the betrayal and cruel murder of the only One who could bear the guilt of His people.

We might also notice that God had instituted three great feasts for His people, feasts that were to be held in Jerusalem by all Israelites.

The first of these was a week-long feast climaxing with the Passover celebration. This meant that for a week, there would have been the maximum number of Jews in Jerusalem (some estimates suggest that this would have been about five times the normal population of the city). It was at the beginning of that week that Jesus made His triumphal entry into Jerusalem, and it was towards the end of that week when He was publicly crucified and then rose again. It was during the next great feast, Pentecost, that the Holy Spirit came. These things were not done in secret. Jesus will return to gather His church and mark the third great feast—when *every* eye shall see Him:

> To him who loves us and has freed us from our sins by his blood and made us a kingdom, priests to his God and Father, to *him be glory and dominion* for ever and ever. Amen. Behold, he is coming with the clouds, and *every eye will see him*, even those who pierced him, and all tribes of the earth will wail on account of him. Even so. Amen. (Revelation 1:5–7; emphasis mine)

There can be no doubt that the sovereign God has had His hand on every detail of the history of the Israelites—and on the rest of history too. History has been referred to as "His story". It is not difficult to see why.

Chapter 3

THE SOVEREIGNTY OF GOD IN INTERNATIONAL AFFAIRS

Suggested Background Reading: Ezra 1

As we look at the way God has dealt with the nations of the earth over the years, we must start by acknowledging that the outcomes of events which appear to be God's purposes may only be a part of what God was doing. There may be many reasons for God's activity which we do not see, or which we may see but do not understand. We must never presume to know the mind of God.

That having been said, we'll start by looking at an event where we are told at least one of the purposes of the event—"that the word of the Lord by the mouth of Jeremiah might be fulfilled" (Ezra 1:1). God had disciplined His people by having them taken into exile, and He had said that the exile would be for a limited time only (seventy years), after which the people would return home.

Jeremiah actually stated at least four times that the people would return, and at least twice he gave the duration of the exile as seventy years.

"Therefore, behold, the days are coming," declares the Lord, "when it shall no longer be said, 'As the Lord lives who brought up the people of Israel out of the land of Egypt', but 'As the Lord lives who brought up the people of Israel out of the north country and out of all the countries where he had driven them.' For I will bring them back to their own land that I gave to their fathers." (Jeremiah 16:14–15)

This whole land shall become a ruin and a waste, and these nations shall serve the king of Babylon seventy years. Then after seventy years are completed, I will punish the king of Babylon and that nation, the land of the Chaldeans, for their iniquity, declares the Lord, making the land an everlasting waste. (Jeremiah 25:11–12)

They shall be carried to Babylon and remain there until the day when I visit them, declares the Lord. Then I will bring them back and restore them to this place. (Jeremiah 27:22)

For thus says the Lord: When seventy years are completed for Babylon, I will visit you, and I will fulfil to you my promise and bring you back to this place. For I know the plans I have for you, declares the Lord, plans for welfare and not for evil, to give you a future and a hope. Then you will call upon me and come and pray to me, and I will hear you. You will seek me and find me, when you seek me with all your heart. I will be found by you, declares the Lord, and I will restore your fortunes and gather you from all the nations and all the places where I have driven you, declares the Lord, and I will bring you back to the place from which I sent you into exile. (Jeremiah 29:10–14)

The Lord was sovereignly bringing to pass the word He had spoken over half a century before.

Daniel was also clear about the length of the exile:

> In the first year of his reign, I, Daniel, perceived in the books the number of years that, according to the word of the Lord to Jeremiah the prophet, must pass before the end of the desolations of Jerusalem, namely, seventy years. (Daniel 9:2)

We are left in no doubt that God was in control of events. We are told that "the Lord stirred up the spirit of Cyrus king of Persia".

The Reformation Study Bible comments on this phrase using the statement "God works sovereignly through responsible human agents to accomplish His redemptive plan." The writer then refers to Solomon's comment in the Proverbs: "The king's heart is a stream of water in the hand of the Lord; He turns it wherever he will" (Proverbs 21:1).

We come back repeatedly to the assurance that the events which brought the exile to an end and which are recorded in the book of Ezra were all within God's sovereign will.

> And they kept the Feast of Unleavened Bread for seven days with joy, for the Lord had made them joyful and had turned the heart of the king of Assyria to them, so that he aided them in the work of the house of God, the God of Israel. (Ezra 6:22)

> Blessed be the Lord, the God of our fathers, who put such a thing as this into the heart of the king, to beautify the house of the Lord that is in Jerusalem, and who extended to me his steadfast love before the king and his counsellors, and before all the king's mighty officers. I took courage, for the hand of the Lord my God was on me, and I gathered leading men from Israel to go up with me. (Ezra 7:27–28)

If we turn our attention to Nehemiah, we see that God was working in his situation too. This is not unexpected because the books of Ezra and Nehemiah were originally a single book. Nevertheless, it is worth noticing the statement that King Artaxerxes was as amenable to the idea of assisting Nehemiah as King Cyrus had been to Ezra, because "the good hand of my God" was upon him.

> And I said to the king, "If it pleases the king, let letters be given to me for the governors of the province Beyond the River, that they may let me pass through until I come to Judah, and a letter to Asaph, the keeper of the king's forest, that he may give me timber to make beams for the gates of the fortress of the temple, and for the wall of the city, and for the house that I shall occupy." And the king granted me what I asked, *for the good hand of my God was upon me.* (Nehemiah 2:7–8; emphasis mine)

God was working through His servants—and in the hearts of pagan kings—to achieve His purposes in a peaceful and dignified way.

One of the outcomes of these events is a situation which lasted well into New Testament times. John spelt it out when he recorded the conversation between Jesus and a Samaritan woman at the well of Sychar: "The Samaritan woman said to him, 'How is it that you, a Jew, ask for a drink from me, a woman of Samaria?'" (for Jews had no dealings with Samaritans) (John 4:9).

When the Jews were taken into exile, a few remained. Other nations, taken into exile from elsewhere, were put into the almost empty cities of Israel, where they intermarried with the remnant. This was the origins of the Samaritans. When Nehemiah came to rebuild Jerusalem, the Samaritans were excluded from the work because they were not pure Jews.

> And I told them [the Jews with Nehemiah] of the hand of my God that had been upon me for good, and also of the words that the king had spoken to me. And they said, "Let us rise up and build." So they strengthened their hands

for the good work. But when Sanballat the Horonite and Tobiah the Ammonite servant and Geshem the Arab heard of it, they jeered at us and despised us and said, "What is this thing that you are doing? Are you rebelling against the king?" Then I replied to them, "The God of heaven will make us prosper, and we his servants will arise and build, but you have no portion or right or claim in Jerusalem." (Nehemiah 2:18–20)

The underlying purpose of God here seems to be the requirement that the Israelites were to be a pure nation and not to intermarry with other nations. God was demanding the loyalty of His people as well as protecting them from the lure of worshipping the false gods of the other nations.

When the Lord your God brings you into the land which you go to possess, and has cast out many nations before you, the Hittites and the Girgashites and the Amorites and the Canaanites and the Perizzites and the Hivites and the Jebusites, seven nations greater and mightier than you, and when the Lord your God delivers them over to you, you shall conquer them and utterly destroy them. You shall make no covenant with them nor show mercy to them. Nor shall you make marriages with them. You shall not give your daughter to their son, nor take their daughter for your son. For they will turn your sons away from following Me, to serve other gods. (Deuteronomy 7:1–4)

Be very careful, therefore, to love the Lord your God. For if you turn back and cling to the remnant of these nations remaining among you and make marriages with them, so that you associate with them and they with you, know for certain that the Lord your God will no longer drive out these nations before you, but they shall be a snare and a trap for you, a whip on your sides and thorns in your eyes, until you perish from off this good ground that the Lord your God has given you. (Joshua 23:11–13)

As we saw earlier, another purpose of God in wanting His people to be a pure nation would presumably be so they would be a picture of the purity of His church. Paul tells us that we should not be in a partnership with those who could cause us to compromise our relationship with God. This is a great example of the eternal plans of a sovereign God using history in Old Testament times to prepare for the coming of His Son.

We read in 2 Corinthians 6:14, "Do not be unequally yoked with unbelievers. For what partnership has righteousness with lawlessness? Or what fellowship has light with darkness?"

Another example of God using His people in His dealings with other nations is the story of Esther. She was an orphan girl in captivity being brought up by her cousin Mordecai.

> Now there was a Jew in Susa the citadel whose name was Mordecai, the son of Jair, son of Shimei, son of Kish, a Benjaminite, who had been carried away from Jerusalem among the captives carried away with Jeconiah king of Judah, whom Nebuchadnezzar king of Babylon had carried away. He was bringing up Hadassah, that is Esther, the daughter of his uncle, for she had neither father nor mother. The young woman had a beautiful figure and was lovely to look at, and when her father and her mother died, Mordecai took her as his own daughter. (Esther 2:5–7)

There are several incidents in this story which at first appear to be of no significance. We are told that Mordecai discovers a plot against the king. He sends a message to the king via Esther, and the plot is foiled and the incident is duly recorded. God makes sure of this recording. When He needs Mordecai to come to prominence, He withdraws sleep from the king. The king then has the record books read to him and is reminded of the incident, and he honours Mordecai. The relationship between the Jews in Susa and the natives of that city are clearly strained, but God allows the Persians to persecute the Jews so that He can have the glory when the leader of the persecution is hanged.

Egypt plays a significant part in biblical history, especially the relationship between the Egyptians and the Israelites. There are three occasions when God's people enter Egypt and live there for a time.

The first is recorded for us in Genesis. At the end of chapter 11, we read of Abram moving from Ur of the Chaldeans to Haran with his family. In chapter 12 we are told that God called him from Haran to the land He was going to make His people's home, but Abram, faced with famine there, journeyed on as far as Egypt. Abram lied that Sarai was his wife, saying she was his sister (she was actually his half-sister), and she was taken to Pharaoh's palace. God intervened to prevent any actual immorality taking place. The couple left Egypt and returned to the land of Canaan, where God made His covenant with Abram.

The relationship between Abram and Pharaoh was quite amicable to start with, but it turned hostile when Pharaoh discovered that Abram had been lying about Sarai.

A similar incident took place later, when Abram (now Abraham) told the same lie about Sarai (now Sarah) to Abimelech, king of Gerar. Once more God ensured that Sarah was not violated. (This is recorded in Genesis 20.)

The second time God's people entered Egypt started when eleven of the sons of Israel sold their brother Joseph into slavery to a caravan of Ishmaelite traders heading for Egypt. This was followed by the whole family moving to Egypt and settling there. They were there for 430 years. The Israelites lived in peace at first, but as they became more numerous, the Egyptians subjected them to slavery, where they remained until God raised Moses up to take them back to the land He had promised them. (The scriptural account starts in Genesis 37 and continues until the Exodus in Exodus 12.)

We need to see God's sovereign hand in these events. Joseph certainly did.

We read in Genesis 50:19–20, "Joseph said to them, 'Do not fear, for am I in the place of God? As for you, you meant evil against me, but *God meant it for good*, to bring it about that many people should be kept alive, as they are today'" (emphasis mine).

Here again, we can see God demonstrating His plans for humankind. He used Moses to bring His people out of slavery to the Egyptians and into a place which He had prepared. The picture is one of Christ bringing His people, the church, out of slavery to sin into the place which He has prepared: "In my Father's house are many rooms. If it were not so, would I have told you that I go to prepare a place for you? And if I go and prepare a place for you, I will come again and will take you to myself, that where I am you may be also" (John 14:2–3).

The link between the Exodus under Moses and the work of Jesus is made clear for us. The third time we read of God's people in Egypt, we see that the people in question were a young couple with a tiny baby—the Son of God Himself—fleeing from the anger of Herod, who had been cheated by the wise men who came to Bethlehem.

Hosea 11:1 reads, "When Israel was a child, I loved him, and out of Egypt I called my son."

> An angel of the Lord appeared to Joseph in a dream and said, "Rise, take the child and his mother, and flee to Egypt, and remain there until I tell you, for Herod is about to search for the child, to destroy him." And he rose and took the child and his mother by night and departed to Egypt and remained there until the death of Herod. This was to

fulfil what the Lord had spoken by the prophet, "Out of Egypt I called my son." (Matthew 2:13–15)

Question 5. *When Hosea prophesied "out of Egypt I have called my Son", was he referring to Abraham, the Israelites under Moses, or Jesus?*

Another important example of how God uses people from heathen nations to fulfil His own purposes for His own nation, the Israelites, is that of Rahab. Before the military invasion of Jericho by the Israelites, God used Rahab to bring great encouragement to His people. We do not know whether the spies sent to Jericho went to Rahab's house not knowing who she was, or if they thought that going to the house of a prostitute would attract less attention and cause less suspicion in a city where they would not be recognised. Either way, they ended up at the house where God had prepared somebody with a message for them. Rahab told the spies that the people of Jericho were terrified of the Israelites—and she told them why. God had also prepared Rahab to protect the spies from the city authorities before helping them to escape. She probably was not the only one in Jericho with a house on the city wall, but God had taken the spies to one of the few of such houses. God was putting His sovereign master plan into action so that He would keep His promise to His people of providing them a homeland.

> And Joshua the son of Nun sent two men secretly from Acacia as spies, saying, "Go, view the land, especially Jericho." And they went and came into the house of a prostitute whose name was Rahab and lodged there. ...
>
> Before the men lay down, she came up to them on the roof and said to the men, "I know that the Lord has given you the land, and that the fear of you has fallen upon us, and that all the inhabitants of the land melt away before you." ...
>
> Then she let them down by a rope through the window, for her house was built into the city wall, so that she lived in the wall. (Joshua 2:1, 8–9, 15)

We also read of God's faithfulness to Rahab in His sparing of her life, and her family, when Jericho fell to the Israelites:

> And the city and all that is within it shall be devoted to the Lord for destruction. Only Rahab the prostitute and all who are with her in her house shall live, because she hid the messengers whom we sent. ...
>
> But to the two men who had spied out the land, Joshua said, "Go into the prostitute's house and bring out from there the woman and all who belong to her, as you swore to her." So the young men who had been spies went in and brought out Rahab and her father and mother and brothers and all who belonged to her. And they brought all her relatives and put them outside the camp of Israel. And they burned the city with fire, and everything in it. Only the silver and gold, and the vessels of bronze and of iron, they put into the treasury of the house of the Lord. But Rahab the prostitute and her father's household and all who belonged to her, Joshua saved alive. And she has lived in Israel to this day, because she hid the messengers whom Joshua sent to spy out Jericho. (Joshua 6:17, 22–25)

Not only was Rahab saved from the destruction of Jericho, but also she was allowed to live in Israel and marry an Israelite. And she was accorded the amazing honour of being one of only four women to be named (a fifth is referred to but not named) in the genealogy of Jesus our Lord. For Matthew to include the names of women in his genealogy was, in itself, a break with tradition, but for a foreign prostitute to be included is quite surprising.

Matthew 1:5–6 reads, "And Salmon the father of Boaz by Rahab, and Boaz the father of Obed by Ruth, and Obed the father of Jesse, and Jesse the father of David the king."

This leads us to ask if God had Rahab's name on this list as an honour or if He had some other purpose for it. Whilst we are not given the answer to this, we may notice that Salmon seems to have disobeyed God's laws by marrying a Gentile, which, as we have noted earlier, was forbidden. One suggestion is that God has given us an example of what conversion is. Someone from outside put his faith in God and so was accepted as part of God's family. Then he could experience salvation and have all the privileges—and responsibilities—of being one of God's people. Ruth was also accepted as one of God's people in the same way.

Question 6. *God's dealings in Jericho led to Rahab's being part of the family tree of Jesus (Matthew 1:5). Did God have a purpose in this?*

One man who had a big influence in a foreign country was Daniel. It is fairly easy to trace the control which God was exercising over events in the life of this man. For example, Daniel was taken into exile when God gave the people into the hand of Nebuchadnezzar.

> In the third year of the reign of Jehoiakim king of Judah, Nebuchadnezzar king of Babylon came to Jerusalem and besieged it. And the Lord gave Jehoiakim king of Judah into his hand, with some of the vessels of the house of God. And he brought them to the land of Shinar, to the house of his god, and placed the vessels in the treasury of his god. (Daniel 1:1–2)

God now had His man in Babylon but wanted him in the king's palace. So God gave Daniel favour. He also gave Daniel and his friends wisdom so that they would be where He wanted them at the right time.

We read in Daniel 1:9, 17, "And God gave Daniel favour and compassion in the sight of the chief of the eunuchs. ... As for these four youths, God gave them learning and skill in all literature and wisdom, and Daniel had understanding in all visions and dreams."

When Daniel was in place and ready, God gave Nebuchadnezzar a dream, and He gave Daniel its meaning (when Daniel prayed about it with his friends).

> Then Daniel went to his house and made the matter known to Hananiah, Mishael, and Azariah, his companions, and told them to seek mercy from the God of heaven concerning this mystery, so that Daniel and his companions might not be destroyed with the rest of the wise men of Babylon. Then the mystery was revealed to Daniel in a vision of the night. Then Daniel blessed the God of heaven. Daniel answered and said: "Blessed be the name of God for ever and ever, to whom belong wisdom and might. He changes times and seasons; he removes kings and sets up kings; he gives wisdom to the wise and knowledge to those who have understanding; he reveals deep and hidden things; he knows what is in the darkness, and the light dwells with him. To you, O God of my fathers, I give thanks and praise, for you have given me wisdom and might, and have now made known to me what we asked of you, for you have made known to us the king's matter." (Daniel 2:17–23)

This, in itself, is a marvellous declaration of the sovereignty of God!

The interpretation of the dream is also about how God would deal with the kingdom over a significant period of time.

> You, O king, the king of kings, to whom the God of heaven has given the kingdom, the power, and the might, and the glory, and into whose hand he has given, wherever they dwell, the children of man, the beasts of the field, and the birds of the heavens, making you rule over them all—you are the head of gold. ... A great God has made known to the king what shall be after this. The dream is certain, and its interpretation sure. (Daniel 2:37–38, 45)

This, with the rest of the meaning of dream, has been seen to have been played out in the history of the Middle East as God unfolded His plan for the region.

God sometimes allows His people to experience difficult situations in order to achieve His purposes in other nations. Two classic examples are found in the book of Daniel which also demonstrate His sovereignty over nature.

Firstly, Daniel's three friends defy the orders of the king to worship a statue. The punishment for this was to be instant cremation, but the friends would not engage in idolatry and trusted God to look after them. They said as much to the king.

> Shadrach, Meshach, and Abednego answered and said to the king, "O Nebuchadnezzar, we have no need to answer you in this matter. If this be so, our God whom we serve is able to deliver us from the burning fiery furnace, and he will deliver us out of your hand, O king. But if not, be it known to you, O king, that we will not serve your gods or worship the golden image that you have set up." (Daniel 3:16–18)

The outcome of this was that King Nebuchadnezzar respected the friends and, therefore, their God. God had shown His sovereignty over fire. The king of the Babylonian empire gave protection to God's people.

> Nebuchadnezzar answered and said, "Blessed be the God of Shadrach, Meshach, and Abednego, who has sent his angel and delivered his servants, who trusted in him, and set aside the king's command, and yielded up their bodies rather than serve and worship any god except their own God. Therefore I make a decree: Any people, nation, or language that speaks anything against the God of Shadrach, Meshach, and Abednego shall be torn limb from limb, and their houses laid in ruins, for there is no other god who is able to rescue in this way." (Daniel 3:28–29)

The second example involves Daniel himself and King Darius:

> All the presidents of the kingdom, the prefects and the
> satraps, the counsellors and the governors are agreed that
> the king should establish an ordinance and enforce an
> injunction, that whoever makes petition to any god or man
> for thirty days, except to you, O king, shall be cast into the
> den of lions. (Daniel 6:7)

Daniel ignored the king and continued to pray to God. The king
reluctantly ordered the punishment for so doing, and Daniel was
thrown to the lions.

We read in Daniel 6:16, "Then the king commanded, and Daniel was
brought and cast into the den of lions. The king declared to Daniel,
'May your God, whom you serve continually, deliver you!'"

Once again, God showed His sovereignty by preventing the lions from
harming Daniel. The outcome was an order from the king that his
entire empire should serve God. King Darius became aware of the
sovereignty of God as he saw what God had done for Daniel.

> Then King Darius wrote to all the peoples, nations, and
> languages that dwell in all the earth: "Peace be multiplied
> to you. I make a decree, that in all my royal dominion
> people are to tremble and fear before the God of Daniel,
> for he is the living God, enduring for ever; his kingdom
> shall never be destroyed, and his dominion shall be to the
> end. He delivers and rescues; he works signs and wonders
> in heaven and on earth, he who has saved Daniel from the
> power of the lions." (Daniel 6:25–27)

Another example of God exercising His sovereignty in an international
setting is found in the life of Solomon. When he asked God for wisdom,
God used His sovereignty over Solomon's mind by giving him that
wisdom. And He gave him much more besides.

"Give your servant therefore an understanding mind to govern your people, that I may discern between good and evil, for who is able to govern this your great people?"

It pleased the Lord that Solomon had asked this. And God said to him, "Because you have asked this, and have not asked for yourself long life or riches or the life of your enemies, but have asked for yourself understanding to discern what is right, behold, I now do according to your word. Behold, I give you a wise and discerning mind, so that none like you has been before you and none like you shall arise after you. I give you also what you have not asked, both riches and honour, so that no other king shall compare with you, all your days." (1 Kings 3:9–13)

The news of this spread around the world so that God's name would be honoured internationally. This is demonstrated by the visit of the Queen of Sheba:

And she said to the king, "The report was true that I heard in my own land of your words and of your wisdom, but I did not believe the reports until I came and my own eyes had seen it. And behold, the half was not told me. Your wisdom and prosperity surpass the report that I heard. Happy are your men! Happy are your servants, who continually stand before you and hear your wisdom! Blessed be the Lord your God, who has delighted in you and set you on the throne of Israel! Because the Lord loved Israel for ever, he has made you king, that you may execute justice and righteousness." (1 Kings 10:6–9)

A New Testament example of God's sovereignty in international affairs is drawn from Paul's missionary journeys. This relates to nations interacting with each other not in a diplomatic or political way, but rather in the way the gospel was spread around the world. The Holy Spirit prevented Paul from going to Asia, and the Spirit of

Jesus stopped him going to Bithynia, but God spoke to him in a dream and directed him to go to Macedonia.

> And they went through the region of Phrygia and Galatia, having been forbidden by the Holy Spirit to speak the word in Asia. And when they had come up to Mysia, they attempted to go into Bithynia, but the Spirit of Jesus did not allow them. So, passing by Mysia, they went down to Troas. And a vision appeared to Paul in the night: a man of Macedonia was standing there, urging him and saying, "Come over to Macedonia and help us." And when Paul had seen the vision, immediately we sought to go on into Macedonia, concluding that God had called us to preach the gospel to them. (Acts 16:6–10)

We can but stand in awe as we see God at work on the world stage. As we look at the world today, we may wonder what He is doing, yet we can be encouraged by the knowledge that, despite the seeming chaos, God is in control of it all.

41

THE SOVEREIGNTY OF
GOD IN WARFARE

Suggested Background Reading: Obadiah and Habakkuk 1–2

In order to put God's display of His sovereignty into context, it would be useful to turn to the prophecies of Obadiah and Habakkuk as two of many examples of God's dealings with the hostilities between nations, and to take a look at the history in which these prophecies were made.

After the death of Solomon, the Kingdom of Israel was split into two separate kingdoms. The northern kingdom of ten tribes kept the name of Israel—though they were sometimes referred to as "Ephraim", especially in prophecies—whereas the Tribe of Judah broke away and were known as such, with Benjamin remaining loyal to them. It is important to remember that it was through Judah that we trace the coming of Jesus.

If we take a big sweep through the history of God's people in the Old Testament, we see time and time again that God had to send—or allow—foreign nations into their midst to punish or discipline them for their sin. These invasions would often be quite severe, but God never allowed the total destruction of the people through whom He had covenanted to send His Messiah. Obadiah is among the prophets who gave assurance of this: "But in Mount Zion there shall be those who escape, and it shall be holy, and the house of Jacob shall possess their own possessions" (Obadiah 17).

God promised that there would always be a remnant through which He would raise up His Messiah, Jesus.

After the kingdom split, there were different kings ruling over each part. In general, the kings of Israel were far more wicked than the kings of Judah, though some of Judah's kings were not to be admired.

The split took place in 931 BC. The two kingdoms lived side by side for just over two hundred years, until the Northern Kingdom of Israel was taken into exile by the Assyrians in 721–722 BC. These ten tribes never returned as such and are often called "the lost tribes of Israel".

Judah, however, remained in the Promised Land until they were invaded by the Babylonians and taken into exile in about 586 BC. These tribes were able to return, rebuild Jerusalem, and resettle the area under Zerubbabel, Ezra, and Nehemiah.

It is this invasion of Jerusalem which Habakkuk was writing about and for which God punished the Babylonians.

Against that background, we take an overview of the prophecy of Obadiah, who is known as "the Prophet of Doom".

This prophecy of Obadiah is set in the period between the Assyrian invasion of Israel and the Babylonian invasion of Judah. He appears to be writing about 700 BC.

The tribe of Edom, who were descended from Esau, lived a nomadic existence in an area south of the Dead Sea. This overlapped with the area which had earlier been occupied by the Moabites and which we shall meet again when we look at the story of Ruth. It is worth noting that the Israelites were descended from Esau's brother, Jacob (whose name was changed to Israel).

The Edomites were known for their many raids on surrounding areas, especially Israel—God's chosen people. Israel and Edom were unable to live peacefully side by side, and the Edomites were thus to be punished by God. Obadiah was sent to warn them of this.

It is a sign of God's grace that, while He justifiably punished His people's enemies, He first sent a warning through His prophet Obadiah.

The message was one of judgement for Edom and the coming day when God would wipe them out as a nation and reestablish the homeland of Israel:

> The house of Jacob shall be a fire, and the house of Joseph a flame, and the house of Esau stubble; they shall burn them and consume them, and there shall be no survivor for the house of Esau, for the Lord has spoken. (Obadiah 18)

So God gave Obadiah a vision about the complete destruction of Edom in return for their aggression towards His people.

Israel's enemies would be destroyed and Israel would be restored in their lands under God's rule. We read in Obadiah 21, "And the kingdom shall be the Lord's."

If we now take an overview of Habakkuk's prophecy, we see something broadly similar, but from a slightly different perspective.

Habakkuk is often referred to as "the Prophet of Doubt and Faith". He was a little later than Obadiah, possibly writing about 605 BC.

Habakkuk prophesied the destruction of Jerusalem, which took place in 586 BC. King Manasseh and others had reinstated the worship of pagan gods such as Baal and Asherah. After the Babylonians had defeated the Assyrians at Nineveh, they turned their attention to Jerusalem. King Zedekiah, the last king of Judah, became a puppet of Nebuchadnezzar. There was a time of uneasy peace. However, Habakkuk predicted the total destruction of Jerusalem.

We are now in a position to use these prophecies in more detail, together with many examples from the historical scriptures, and consider more carefully how God is ensuring that His plans are being brought about as, in His sovereignty, He directs the nations.

We saw in the prophecy of Obadiah that God determined to punish Edom. The sibling rivalry between Esau and Jacob went right back to their early days, even before they were born. We read in Genesis 25:23, "And the Lord said to her, 'Two nations are in your womb, and two peoples from within you shall be divided; the one shall be stronger than the other, the older shall serve the younger.'"

Then we read of Esau selling his birthright for a portion of stew:

> Once when Jacob was cooking stew, Esau came in from the field, and he was exhausted. And Esau said to Jacob, "Let me eat some of that red stew, for I am exhausted!" (Therefore his name was called Edom.) Jacob said, "Sell me your birthright now." Esau said, "I am about to die; of what use is a birthright to me?" Jacob said, "Swear to me now." So he swore to him and sold his birthright to Jacob. Then Jacob gave Esau bread and lentil stew, and he ate and drank and rose and went his way. Thus Esau despised his birthright. (Genesis 25:29–34)

Jacob also cheated Esau out of their father's blessing.

> His father Isaac said to him, "Who are you?" He answered, "I am your son, your firstborn, Esau." Then Isaac trembled very violently and said, "Who was it then that hunted game

and brought it to me, and I ate it all before you came, and I have blessed him? Yes, and he shall be blessed." (Genesis 27:32–33)

This resulted in Jacob becoming afraid of Esau. The divisions between them lasted down through the generations.

> And the messengers returned to Jacob, saying, "We came to your brother Esau, and he is coming to meet you, and there are four hundred men with him." Then Jacob was greatly afraid and distressed. He divided the people who were with him, and the flocks and herds and camels, into two camps, thinking, "If Esau comes to one camp and attacks it, then the camp that is left will escape." (Genesis 32:6–8)

When the children of Israel (i.e. the descendants of Jacob) left Egypt, heading for the Promised Land, they wanted to pass through Edom, but the Edomites (i.e. the descendants of Esau) refused to let them pass.

Moses and the Israelite people twice appealed to their common ancestry and asked the king of Edom for passage through his land along the "King's Highway", on their way to Canaan, but the king refused permission. Accordingly, they detoured around the country either because of his show of force or because God had ordered them to do so rather than wage war. The king of Edom did not attack the Israelites, though he prepared to resist any aggression on their part.

> Moses sent messengers from Kadesh to the king of Edom: "Thus says your brother Israel: You know all the hardship that we have met: how our fathers went down to Egypt, and we lived in Egypt for a long time. And the Egyptians dealt harshly with us and our fathers. And when we cried to the Lord, he heard our voice and sent an angel and brought us out of Egypt. And here we are in Kadesh, a city on the edge of your territory. Please let us pass through your land.

We will not pass through field or vineyard, or drink water from a well. We will go along the King's Highway. We will not turn aside to the right hand or to the left until we have passed through your territory." But Edom said to him, "You shall not pass through, lest I come out with the sword against you." And the people of Israel said to him, "We will go up by the highway, and if we drink of your water, I and my livestock, then I will pay for it. Let me only pass through on foot, nothing more." But he said, "You shall not pass through." And Edom came out against them with a large army and with a strong force. Thus Edom refused to give Israel passage through his territory, so Israel turned away from him. (Numbers 20:14–21)

When the time did come for the Israelites to pass through Edom, God was very careful to avoid military conflict. He had other plans for dealing with the Edomites. His people were weary from travelling, were not trained in warfare, and were ill-equipped.

You have been travelling around this mountain country long enough. Turn northwards and command the people, "You are about to pass through the territory of your brothers, the people of Esau, who live in Seir; and they will be afraid of you. So be very careful. Do not contend with them, for I will not give you any of their land, no, not so much as for the sole of the foot to tread on, because I have given Mount Seir to Esau as a possession. You shall purchase food from them for money, that you may eat, and you shall also buy water of them for money, that you may drink." (Deuteronomy 2:3–6)

Question 7. *God gave the Promised Land to the Israelites, but He also gave land to the Edomites (Deuteronomy 2:3–6). Does knowing this change how we think about the stories of Moses and Joshua?*

Question 8. *Why do the Edomites not live there now?*

Even after the Israelites entered their Promised Land and settled down, their relationship with neighbouring nations did not improve.

In the time of Nebuchadnezzar II, the Edomites helped plunder Jerusalem and slaughter the Judeans. For this reason, the prophets denounced Edom violently, and with the psalmist, they prophesied, or called on God for, revenge.

> Remember, O Lord, against the Edomites the day of Jerusalem, how they said, "Lay it bare, lay it bare, down to its foundations!" (Psalm 137:7)

> For the Lord has a day of vengeance, a year of recompense for the cause of Zion. And the streams of Edom shall be turned into pitch, and her soil into sulphur; her land shall become burning pitch. Night and day it shall not be quenched; its smoke shall go up for ever. From generation to generation it shall lie waste; none shall pass through it for ever and ever. (Isaiah 34:8–10)

> Concerning Edom. Thus says the Lord of hosts: "Is wisdom no more in Teman? Has counsel perished from the prudent? Has their wisdom vanished? Flee, turn back, dwell in the depths, O inhabitants of Dedan! For I will bring the calamity of Esau upon him, the time when I punish him. If grape-gatherers came to you, would they not leave gleanings? If thieves came by night, would they not destroy only enough for themselves? But I have stripped Esau bare; I have uncovered his hiding places, and he is not able to conceal himself. His children are destroyed, and his brothers, and his neighbours; and he is no more." (Jeremiah 49:7–10)

Recent archaeological investigations have shown that the country flourished between the thirteenth and the eighth century BC and was destroyed by the Babylonians after a period of decline in the sixth century BC.

It appears that the few Edomites who escaped from the Babylonians moved north and west into Idumea before disappearing without trace.

The last unambiguous reference to Edom is an Assyrian inscription of 667 BC; it has thus been unclear when, how, and why Edom ceased to exist as a state, other than the scriptural references in the book of Obadiah where he explains this fact.

So, let us consider the sovereignty of God in all this:

- God had kept His people free from conflict with the Edomites in the time of Moses.
- God had kept His people free from conflict with the Edomites when the final punishment of Esau came.
- God used the Babylonians to execute His judgement, even though they were not "His" people. They were a barbarian race who had no time for God, but they did God's bidding without realising it.
- God used Obadiah to warn the Edomites of the coming judgement, even giving the reason "Because of the violence done to your brother Jacob" (Obadiah 10).

The book of Habakkuk records a conversation which he had with God. In chapter 1, Habakkuk complains that God has not judged the sin, violence, and injustice which is around him. God replies that He is going to use the Babylonians to do this. Habakkuk is horrified and complains to God that the Babylonians are even worse than God's unfaithful people. Clearly, God is already aware of this

For behold, I am raising up the Chaldeans, that bitter and hasty nation, who march through the breadth of the earth, to seize dwellings not their own. They are dreaded and fearsome; their justice and dignity go forth from themselves. (Habakkuk 1:6–7)

In chapter 2, God replies that they, too, will be judged for attacking His people. There is no escape from God as their idols are worthless and unable to act, whereas God is living and powerful.

Habakkuk's book ends (chapter 3) with a prayer of submission to God. He prays for mercy and lists God's mighty acts of deliverance in history. He will wait for God's salvation with joy and trust.

It is quite remarkable that God used a nation such as the Babylonians to carry out His directions, but as we see in Habakkuk's prophecy, He used them to discipline His own people, but then He also punished the Babylonians for attacking His people.

The Babylonian Chronicles, held in the British Museum in London, tell us the following:

> In the seventh year of Nebuchadnezzar, 598 BC, in the month Chislev [November–December], the king of Babylon assembled his army, and after he had invaded the land of Hatti [Syria/Palestine] he laid siege to the city of Judah. On the second day of the month of Adar [16 March] he conquered the city and took the king [King Jeconiah] prisoner. He installed in his place a puppet king [King Zedekiah] of his own choice, and after he had received rich tribute, he sent forth to Babylon.

This document is a secular piece of writing, but it fits well with the scriptural account of the events of the time.

There has been some debate as to when the second siege of Jerusalem took place. There is no dispute that Jerusalem fell the second time in the summer month of Tammuz ("On the ninth day of the fourth month the famine was so severe in the city that there was no food for the people of the land" (Jeremiah 52:6)). The debate is about the year in which the end of Zedekiah's reign and the fall of Jerusalem occurred. Some historians quote 586 BC; others, 587 BC.

Habakkuk's frustration is about the lack of discipline among God's own people. This is right up to date as we see evil all around us today and wonder why God doesn't do something about it. The reassuring answer is that God has a plan to punish sin, and He explains to Habakkuk what that plan is. The Chaldeans, another name for the Babylonians, were waiting in the wings as God was about to send them to Jerusalem. First, God gave Habakkuk the warning of His action so that those who were faithful to Him would have the opportunity to escape and live (2:4). God was planning events for His own glory (2:14).

Behold, his soul is puffed up; it is not upright within him, but the righteous shall live by his faith. … For the earth will be filled with the knowledge of the glory of the Lord as the waters cover the sea. (Habakkuk 2:4, 14)

Once more we see the sovereignty of God in these events.

- It is clear that God had a plan to punish His people.
- It is clear that God had a plan to use the prophecy of Habakkuk to warn His people of their judgement.
- It is clear that God had a plan to punish the Babylonians.
- It is also clear that God, in His sovereignty, was able to put all these plans into action.

One of the clearest indications of God's sovereignty in warfare is described for us in Exodus. Israel is being attacked by the Amalekites, and Moses sends Joshua to repel them. When Moses, with the "staff of God" in his hand, raises his arms in the attitude of prayer, the Israelites push forward, but when he lowers them, the Amalekites fight back.

Then Amalek came and fought with Israel at Rephidim. So Moses said to Joshua, "Choose for us men, and go out and fight with Amalek. Tomorrow I will stand on the top of the hill with the staff of God in my hand." So Joshua did as Moses told him, and fought with Amalek, while Moses,

> Aaron, and Hur went up to the top of the hill. Whenever
> Moses held up his hand, Israel prevailed, and whenever
> he lowered his hand, Amalek prevailed. (Exodus 17:8–11)

This demonstrates not only that God was directing the battle but He also directs us, His soldiers, signalling that we need to be constantly in prayer.

Another clear indication of God's sovereignty in warfare is found at the end of King Saul's life. The Israelites were being threatened by the Philistines, and Saul was afraid. He had disobeyed God, so when he turned to God for advice, he received no answer. In desperation, he turned to witchcraft—strictly forbidden by God.

Leviticus 19:31 reads, "Do not turn to mediums or necromancers; do not seek them out, and so make yourselves unclean by them: I am the Lord your God."

Leviticus 20:6 tells us, "If a person turns to mediums and necromancers, whoring after them, I will set my face against that person and will cut him off from among his people."

We know that Saul was aware of this because he had proscribed witchcraft in Israel. Thus when he spoke to Samuel through the medium, he should not have been surprised to learn of God's punishment on him, including his own death.

> Now Samuel had died, and all Israel had mourned for him
> and buried him in Ramah, his own city. And Saul had put
> the mediums and the necromancers out of the land. The
> Philistines assembled and came and encamped at Shunem.
> And Saul gathered all Israel, and they encamped at Gilboa.
> When Saul saw the army of the Philistines, he was afraid,
> and his heart trembled greatly. And when Saul enquired of
> the Lord, the Lord did not answer him, either by dreams,

or by Urim, or by prophets. Then Saul said to his servants, "Seek out for me a woman who is a medium, that I may go to her and enquire of her." And his servants said to him, "Behold, there is a medium at En-dor." ...

Then the woman said, "Whom shall I bring up for you?"

He said, "Bring up Samuel for me." ...

Then Samuel said to Saul, ... "The Lord will give Israel also with you into the hand of the Philistines, and tomorrow you and your sons shall be with me. The Lord will give the army of Israel also into the hand of the Philistines." (1 Samuel 28:3–7, 11, 15, 19)

Question 9. *Why did God forbid witchcraft (Leviticus 19 and 20)?*

Once more, God's sovereign will was foretold and His plans came to pass in full. Saul's death, together with the deaths of his three sons and his armour-bearer, was part of a great defeat of Saul's army, while David was routing the Amalekites.

A well-known example of God fighting battles for His people is the account of the defeat of Jericho. This was one of the first main battles fought by the Israelites as they entered the Promised Land. Here, God showed His people that He would act on their behalf if they trusted Him. The method of fighting was unorthodox to say the least. The army simply marched round the city a total of thirteen times, and then the city was theirs for the taking.

So the people shouted, and the trumpets were blown. As soon as the people heard the sound of the trumpet, the people shouted a great shout, and the wall fell down flat, so that the people went up into the city, every man straight before him, and they captured the city. (Joshua 6:20)

The omnipotent God had provided a victory which would not have been possible by human power alone.

Another example of God showing His power on the battlefield is the victory given to Gideon. Once more, the victory depended on Gideon and his men following God's instructions. God had determined the fate of the Midianites and was demonstrating His power by reducing Gideon's army to just three hundred men and then arming them with trumpets—not the usual weapon of war!

There could have been at least three reasons for reducing Gideon's army from thirty-two thousand, to ten thousand, to three hundred.

Firstly, there were twenty-two thousand men who were afraid of the battle. God allowed these men to leave the scene because their fear told of a lack of trust in Him, and they were not to be part of the drama.

Secondly, there were nine thousand seven hundred men who were not fit to be soldiers. They lapped water from the river in a way which left them vulnerable to a surprise attack. The three hundred who scooped water up in their hands were able to keep watch on the surrounding area at the same time. God wanted these men to be His representatives in the battle.

Thirdly, with a small group of men, rather than a large army, it would be clear that God was fighting the battle—and He would have all the glory.

> The Lord said to Gideon, "The people with you are too many for me to give the Midianites into their hand, lest Israel boast over me, saying, 'My own hand has saved me.' Now therefore proclaim in the ears of the people, saying, 'Whoever is fearful and trembling, let him return home and hurry away from Mount Gilead.'" Then 22,000 of the people returned, and 10,000 remained. ... So the people took provisions in their hands, and their trumpets. And he

54

sent all the rest of Israel every man to his tent, but retained the 300 men. And the camp of Midian was below him in the valley. ... And they cried out, "A sword for the Lord and for Gideon!" Every man stood in his place around the camp, and all the army ran. They cried out and fled. When they blew the 300 trumpets, the Lord set every man's sword against his comrade and against all the army. And the army fled. (Judges 7:2–3, 8, 20–22)

Some battles in scripture were fought and won very decisively without a single arrow being removed from its quiver or a single sword being drawn. Maybe the clearest example of this is found in the account of the Israelites' escape from the Egyptians at the Red Sea.

First, God set a trap for the Egyptians.

Then the Lord said to Moses, "Tell the people of Israel to turn back and encamp in front of Pi-hahiroth, between Migdol and the sea, in front of Baal-zephon; you shall encamp facing it, by the sea. For Pharaoh will say of the people of Israel, 'They are wandering in the land; the wilderness has shut them in.' And *I will harden Pharaoh's heart,* and he will pursue them, and I will get glory over Pharaoh and all his host, and *the Egyptians shall know that I am the Lord.*" And they did so. (Exodus 14:1–4; emphasis mine)

God then gave Moses some words of encouragement and told him what to do. Moses was told to lift his staff over the sea, then God would make a path through it. This did not require that Moses do anything difficult or demanding, but it did mean that he had to trust that God could—and would—act to save the Israelites.

The Lord said to Moses, "Why do you cry to me? Tell the people of Israel to go forward. Lift up your staff, and stretch out your hand over the sea and divide it, that the people of

> Israel may go through the sea on dry ground. And I will harden the hearts of the Egyptians so that they shall go in after them, and I will get glory over Pharaoh and all his host, his chariots, and his horsemen. And the Egyptians shall know that I am the Lord, when I have gained glory over Pharaoh, his chariots, and his horsemen." (Exodus 14:15–18)

We are told that Moses did what God instructed him to, and God was true to His word.

> Then Moses stretched out his hand over the sea, and the Lord drove the sea back by a strong east wind all night and made the sea dry land, and the waters were divided. And the people of Israel went into the midst of the sea on dry ground, the waters being a wall to them on their right hand and on their left. The Egyptians pursued and went in after them into the midst of the sea, all Pharaoh's horses, his chariots, and his horsemen. (Exodus 14:21–23)

When Moses obeyed God, God showed His sovereignty in warfare by using His sovereignty over His creation. This is where we go next:

> So Moses stretched out his hand over the sea, and the sea returned to its normal course when the morning appeared. And as the Egyptians fled into it, the Lord threw the Egyptians into the midst of the sea. The waters returned and covered the chariots and the horsemen; of all the host of Pharaoh that had followed them into the sea, not one of them remained. (Exodus 14:27–28)

Here, again, we can notice that the name of God in the Bible is sometimes given as "the Lord of Hosts" or "the God of Hosts". This name speaks of the power and authority of YHVH Sabaoth.

While YHVH Sabaoth can be seen as an intimate God who is with us in the details of our human experience (as He was with Hannah, the mother of Samuel, in her plight of barrenness), He is also a warrior God who commands armies on behalf of His people.

Imagine trying to fight against God! It seems impossible, yet many do it, for example Goliath of the Philistine army.

With weapons in hand, ready for warfare, he issued God's people a challenge: "And the Philistine said, 'I defy the ranks of Israel this day. Give me a man, that we may fight together'" (1 Samuel 17:10).

David responded by declaring his faith in God: "Then David said to the Philistine, 'You come to me with a sword and with a spear and with a javelin, but I come to you in the name of the Lord of Hosts, the God of the armies of Israel, whom you have defied'" (1 Samuel 17:45).

While Goliath openly defied the greatness of Israel's armies, David reminded him that he was coming in the name of the God of Israel's armies; and in doing so, the will of God to defeat the giant Goliath was accomplished.

THE SOVEREIGNTY OF GOD IN CREATION

Suggested Background Reading:
Genesis 1–2, Revelation 4, and the extracts from
commentaries to be found in the appendix

C reation is amazing! Before creation, the triune God dwelt alone in sovereign majesty. He could have chosen not to create anything, but He chose to create the universe according to His own good pleasure. The universe He created is vastly greater and vastly more beautiful than it needed to be. The pinnacle of creation is humankind, created in God's own image (Genesis 1:27) and given an extra dimension to life, that is the spiritual life breathed into their nostrils (Genesis 2:7).

The balance of life is truly amazing, the levels of oxygen and carbon dioxide in the earth's atmosphere being kept in balance by plants turning carbon dioxide into oxygen and animals doing the reverse, thus all of them being able to live. The diversity of creation is also bewildering. Creation has a graduation of size from viruses to blue whales. There are many types of trees, whereas we only need one or two. This all adds greatly to the beauty of our world and to the variety of our diet.

The enormous scale of the universe may leave us wondering if there is life on any other planet, whether any such beings have also been created in the image of God, and if so, whether or not they had a fall such as Adam and Eve brought about in the Garden of Eden. The implications of these questions lead only to speculation, other than reminding us that God, in His sovereignty, knows what He is doing and that He has the answers.

If you were to ask a number of Christians about the origins of the earth, you would probably be given a number of different ideas. There would be some who take the first two chapters of Genesis absolutely literally, saying that God created the universe in six periods of what we now know as twenty-four hours. Other folks would tell you of a Big Bang followed by a process of evolution. There might be a range of ideas about the extent to which God was in control of either the Big Bang or the ensuing evolution.

It is also likely that you would hear a variety of theories which include different elements of the first two answers.

Apart from these strongly held positions, there would be some who have never really bothered to think about where we came from. We are here, and that is all that matters. ("What my birth certificate says is of little importance. I know that I have been born.")

To make progress in our thinking about how the earth started, we need to look at scripture first, and then we can see how this fits with science and our general observations. Coming to a reliable conclusion depends on our asking the right questions and being prepared to accept the answers.

The first question to ask about the first chapters of Genesis is "What are they trying to tell us?" The usual answer to this question is that they are telling us how God created Earth. Unfortunately, that answer is the source of many of our problems.

59

This subject is much easier to discuss when we change that answer from "how" to "why" or "who".

It is true that we are told how in as much as "God said, 'let there be …' and there was …." But the main purpose of the biblical account of creation is surely to tell us that *God* created the earth as a place for Him to put the jewel of His creation, namely the human race. This was to be a place where He could meet with humankind and commune with us. The mechanism by which He did so was of no real importance.

To illustrate the difference between the two approaches, consider an electric kettle as it heats some water.

The question could be asked, "Why is the kettle heating the water?"

The first answer might be about electricity flowing in the wire of the heating element, which is creating heat, which is being transferred to the water.

The second answer could easily be simply "I wanted a cup of coffee!"

The first answer would be relevant if there were discussion about whether the kettle was electric or had been put on a gas hob, over a wood fire, etc., whereas the second answer is for those to whom the means of heating is irrelevant and who are just interested in the purpose of heating the water. One would suggest that Genesis 1–2— along with many other parts of scripture—gives us the second type of answer on this issue.

One of the main arguments is about the meaning of the word *day* in the first two chapters of Genesis.

The Bible never sets out to be a scientific text. It is always supported by science when it is relevant to do so, which is clearly *not* when miracles are being described. Creation has to be one of the greatest of miracles. A much greater miracle—*the greatest miracle*—is our means of salvation, which, happily, does not in any way depend on the length of time taken for Creation!

Arguing over the length of time God spent creating the earth misses the point, especially as God is outside time. The point is that God created a place for His ultimate creation—humankind. For example, in Psalm 90:4 we read, "For a thousand years in your sight are but as yesterday when it is past, or as a watch in the night." And in 2 Peter 3:8 we read, "But do not overlook this one fact, beloved, that with the Lord one day is as a thousand years, and a thousand years as one day."

The arguments continue, however, so it may help to further address the issue.

For some years now, I have had the privilege of helping students prepare for examinations. Many of the younger ones have asked me what GCSEs I took at school. When this first happened, I gave an answer, almost without thinking, which I have since used each time: "We did not have GCSEs in my day. We had O levels." Never has a student challenged the idea that I did all my O levels in one twenty-four-hour period; they all understood that the word *day* was used figuratively. Scripture uses the word figuratively too when referring to the Day of the Lord. (This phrase rings through the Minor Prophets!) Jesus talks about His hour coming in a similar way.

It is also difficult to be sure what a solar day was at the start. We define a day as the time it takes for the earth to complete one revolution on its axis. Genesis 1:2 tells us, "The earth was without form, and void; and darkness was on the face of the deep."

To describe this amorphous swirling mass as rotating on its axis in a clearly defined way stretches the imagination a little. We should also remind ourselves that talking about "solar days" poses serious problems for the first three days of Creation as there was no sun.

(Time is now defined in a rather different way, using atomic activity, but does this not affect the issue?) One could also ask, if a day is twenty-four hours, then how long is a night? The first few verses of Genesis tell us that God separated light, which He called "day", from darkness, which He called "night".

Another comment about time spans concerns a significant change which God made to His creation. In the early days, human beings were able to live hundreds of years. Methuselah topped the list at 969 years of age (Genesis 5:27). Subsequent to that, God put a limit on human life of 120 years (Genesis 6:3). What we are not told is how God brought this change about. The most likely explanation is that God redesigned human metabolism to run at a faster rate (some eight times faster). We know that different species live at different speeds from us—most are rather faster (for example, dogs live about seven times faster than we do, though elephants live at half our speed, and so forth)—so this is possible. There is, however, another possibility, namely that time itself increased in pace—again by a factor of about eight. This would easily explain all that we know about the changes that took place, but at the same time it would alter our perspective on those early events. This possibility must, at the very least, make any calculations of early time unreliable since we cannot be certain about the initial speed of rotation of the earth.

An example of God altering time is an event usually referred to as Joshua's long day, recorded for us in Joshua 10:12–13:

> At that time Joshua spoke to the Lord in the day when the Lord gave the Amorites over to the sons of Israel, and he said in the sight of Israel, "Sun, stand still at Gibeon, and moon, in the Valley of Aijalon." And the sun stood still, and the moon stopped, until the nation took vengeance on their enemies. Is this not written in the Book of Jashar? The sun stopped in the midst of heaven and did not hurry to set for about a whole day.

A similar example is found in the story of King Hezekiah:

> And Isaiah said, "This shall be the sign to you from the Lord, that the Lord will do the thing that he has promised: shall the shadow go forward ten steps, or go back ten steps?" And Hezekiah answered, "It is an easy thing for the shadow to lengthen ten steps. Rather let the shadow go back ten steps." And Isaiah the prophet called to the Lord, and he brought the shadow back ten steps, by which it had gone down on the steps of Ahaz. (2 Kings 20:9–11)

We might also think about the use of language in Genesis.

A few yards from my house is a road sign. It has a picture of two children—one a girl of about seven, the other a boy of about five—below which is the word *school*. Apart from a few occasions during the time when my own children went to the school, the late 1980s, I have never seen two children around those ages anywhere in the area. The dogmatist would say that there must be children of that age here somewhere. If I don't believe that, then I am unfaithful to the sign. The nondogmatist would say that it means that this is an area where children are more likely to be found than elsewhere. In this case we instinctively treat the word *school* as literal and the picture above it as purely figurative. If we are to treat the whole of scripture as absolutely literal, then we will have massive problems with a number of parts of it, not least of which would be the book of Revelation!

Question 10. *God could have made a world in which there were two or three types of tree, but we have an enormous variety of trees. Why might He have done this? You could ask the same question about flowers, animals, etc.*

Some of the other arguments put forward by those who favour the short timescale for Creation are as follows, together with my responses:

Statement 1. We are told that for Calvin and for all the Reformers, a simple plain reading of the Creation account was normal. This interpretation was the generally accepted (but not universally accepted) approach of Christ's church throughout the ages until the middle of the nineteenth century.

Response. A plain simple reading is generally best, but this does not call for blind literalism. The plain simple reading of a School sign does not involve looking for a pair of children such as those pictured. It should also be noted that it was the middle of the nineteenth century when Darwin published his thesis on evolution and caused the church to think about what the text in Genesis was actually saying. Prior to the Reformation, the generally accepted view of scripture was not accepted by Calvin and the Reformers.

Statement 2. We ought to look at what Calvin wrote: "What Moses recounts, that the building of the world was not accomplished in a minute but in six days, tends to the same conclusion as previously stated. For this very circumstance withdraws us from all erroneous imaginations to draw us all the closer to the only God who accomplished his labour in six days so as to free us from the trouble of bothering ourselves all our lives in considering the nature of his creative acts" (John Calvin, *Institutes*, 1:14:2, translated by Jean-Marc Berthoud).

Response. Perspectives may have been different in John Calvin's day (!), but we are not now free from the trouble of bothering ourselves about how literally to understand the word *day*. Furthermore, if we free ourselves "from the trouble of bothering ourselves all our lives in considering the nature of his creative acts", then we run the risk of not bothering ourselves to stand in awe at the majesty and beauty of Creation and at the sovereign power and greatness of the Creator.

Statement 3. Jean-Marc Berthoud (who translated the quotation from Calvin above) wrote a letter to Professor Donald MacLeod. In it he wrote the following:

> The processes which prevail in created nature are not
> the same as those which were used by God to create the

Response. The context of this verse is about believing in the saving of the soul (Hebrews 10:39). This moves the priority of our faith to more essential matters, though belief in God as Creator comes with that. There is no timescale alluded to here. Whatever we believe, let us not be distracted from the central issue of salvation by way of repentance and faith by arguments.

Statement 12. We may be told that those who do not have faith will inevitably "suppress the truth in unrighteousness", just as the Bible says (Romans 1:18). This is what we see in almost every modern debate on this subject.

Response. True—but faith in what (or whom)? Are we asking that men and women should have faith in literalism and solar days of Creation, or in the saving work of Christ at Calvary?

Having read this far, you are probably convinced that it was written by an old-earther. Actually, I am of the opinion that the "days" of Genesis were probably not solar (half of them having no sun), but I read nothing in scripture to suggest that they were any particular length. Their length seems to have no theological importance at all. There are, however, other considerations which affect the Creation-evolution debate.

First Consideration

There are many stars and galaxies which are a long way away. We know from measurements on earth and from telescopes in space that there are many stars which are millions of miles away. If we take the commonly accepted values for the age and the size of the universe, we come to one or more of three conclusions:

- Firstly, the Big Bang theory could be wrong because the universe has not had time to reach its current size, even if stars could travel close to the speed of light. Therefore, God must have created those stars in, or close to, their current positions.

- Secondly, the speed of light might have changed dramatically at some point during the course of time, or else matter used to be able to travel faster than light, which is certainly not possible now.
- Thirdly, God created stars more than six thousand light years away from us. If the act of Creation was just six thousand years ago, the light from those stars must have been well on its journey towards Earth before those stars were created.

Second Consideration

If we were to follow the theory of evolution put forward by Charles Darwin and others, we could calculate the volume of the primordial soup in which life is said to have started. Each step of this calculation will have a range of values, but a conclusion can be reached to find the minimum possible size of the soup by taking values at whichever end of each range of values which favours the evolutionist. The resulting volume would be a sphere with a diameter of roughly sixty-five thousand light years, making it some ten million times the volume of the Milky Way—the galaxy in which our solar system is found!

Third Consideration

There is a scientific law which contradicts the whole theory of evolution. The second law of thermodynamics states that the entropy of an isolated system not in equilibrium will tend to increase over time, approaching a maximum value at equilibrium. (Essentially entropy is the measure of disorder and randomness in a system.) In other words, if left to its own devices, everything goes from bad to worse! In effect, this means that evolution should work backwards and living organisms should become less sophisticated with time, not develop into something more complex.

Fourth Consideration

For evolution to be able to describe the variety of species we observe today, it has to account for a very large number of transitions between species. Each of these transitions should have left evidence in the form of partly changed organisms. In short, there should be a smooth series of very small changes from one to the next. Since these are not found, we have a large number of missing links. The fact that we share about 95 per cent of our DNA with a monkey does not prove that we evolved from monkeys. We share 50 per cent of our DNA with a banana!

Fifth Consideration
The context of the Hebrew word for day, *yom*, does not require a literal meaning.

Additional Thoughts on the Days of Creation
Many commentators have considered the book of Genesis in their writing about the account of creation.

Although it must be borne in mind that commentaries do not have the authority of scripture, it is worth noting that commentators are in general agreement with the idea that the days of Creation should not be taken literally. The appendix contains extracts of the relevant sections of a number of commentaries. These have not been edited to try to twist the meanings!

The extracts are given in no particular order, except that Matthew Henry's has been put first since he wrote his commentary before Charles Darwin published *On the Origin of Species* in 1859, and Charles Ellicott follows since he wrote fairly shortly after Darwin.

Before 1859, nobody seemed to question the use of the word *day* when considering the days of Creation. The length of a day was of no importance anyway. When the theory of evolution threatened to undermine the creative work of God, the church, unfortunately, picked the wrong fight. Evolution should be rejected on the basis that it is bad science and because it is not able to account for the variety of species we see today. Evolution should not be challenged by treating the days of Creation literally and claiming that the timescale is too short for evolution to have taken place.

The sovereignty of God in Creation is beyond doubt.

Question 11. *Do you think that God created* **you** *directly during the events of Genesis 1–2 or as a result of processes started at that time, or at a time nine months or so before you were born, or some other time? Or are you purely an accident?*

The Important Issue

One fact that is obvious from scripture is that God, as Creator, remains master of His creation.

His sovereignty over Creation is demonstrated throughout scripture. A number of examples will illustrate this. This list is in no way intended to be exhaustive:

> Of the birds according to their kinds, and of the animals according to their kinds, of every creeping thing of the ground, according to its kind, two of every sort shall come in to you to keep them alive. (Genesis 6:20, in which God is speaking to Noah)

> On that day all the fountains of the great deep burst forth, and the windows of the heavens were opened. And rain fell upon the earth for forty days and forty nights. On the very same day Noah and his sons, Shem and Ham and Japheth, and Noah's wife and the three wives of his sons with them entered the ark. (Genesis 7:11–13)

> Then the Lord said to Moses and Aaron, "When Pharaoh says to you, 'Prove yourselves by working a miracle,' then you shall say to Aaron, 'Take your staff and cast it down before Pharaoh, that it may become a serpent.'" (Exodus 7:8–9)

The ten plagues of Egypt also apply here.

> Then the Lord opened the mouth of the donkey, and she said to Balaam, "What have I done to you, that you have struck me these three times?" (Numbers 22:28)

Joshua's "long day" has already been noted above.

> [God said,] "You shall drink from the brook, and I have commanded the ravens to feed you there." So he went and did according to the word of the Lord. He went and lived by the brook Cherith that is east of the Jordan. And the ravens brought him bread and meat in the morning, and bread and meat in the evening, and he drank from the brook. (1 Kings 17:4–6)

> But as one was felling a log, his axe head fell into the water, and he cried out, "Alas, my master! It was borrowed." Then the man of God said, "Where did it fall?" When he showed him the place, he cut off a stick and threw it in there and made the iron float. And he said, "Take it up." So, he reached out his hand and took it. (2 Kings 6:5–7)

> And Isaiah said, "This shall be the sign to you from the Lord, that the Lord will do the thing that he has promised: shall the shadow go forward ten steps, or go back ten steps?" And Hezekiah answered, "It is an easy thing for the shadow to lengthen ten steps. Rather let the shadow go back ten steps." And Isaiah the prophet called to the Lord, and he brought the shadow back ten steps, by which it had gone down on the steps of Ahaz. (2 Kings 20:9–11)

Note that this last event and Joshua's long day have both been verified by Harold Hill of the Curtis Engine Company. He is also a consultant in the United States space program using computer software which plotted the positions of the sun, moon, and planets over thousands of years, past and future. All was well until there was a discrepancy when they reached the times of these events. The biblical accounts were applied to the calculations, which brought everything exactly into line. They were calculating in minutes.

But the Lord hurled a great wind upon the sea, and there was a mighty tempest on the sea, so that the ship threatened to break up. ... So they picked up Jonah and hurled him into the sea, and the sea ceased from its raging. (Jonah 1:4, 15)

And the Lord spoke to the fish, and it vomited Jonah out upon the dry land. (Jonah 2:10)

Now the Lord God appointed a plant and made it come up over Jonah, that it might be a shade over his head, to save him from his discomfort. So Jonah was exceedingly glad because of the plant. But when dawn came up the next day, God appointed a worm that attacked the plant, so that it withered. (Jonah 4:6–7)

And he said to them, "Why are you afraid, O you of little faith?" Then he rose and rebuked the winds and the sea, and there was a great calm. (Matthew 8:26)

And in the fourth watch of the night he came to them, walking on the sea. (Matthew 14:25)

"And when they got into the boat, the wind ceased." (Matthew 14:32)

All the healing miracles of Jesus could be added to this list.

Conclusion

In order to reach a clear conclusion, we have to accept four statements: (1) Creation is a work of God which He undertook of His own sovereign will. (2) The timescale of Genesis is *not* relevant to our salvation through the blood of Christ. (3) Evolution is a phenomenon which does exist, but which can *never* replace Creation. (4) Evolution accounts for changes *within* a species (new diseases etc.), but no more.

We could ask ourselves two questions:

- Did God create the Ebola virus and COVID-19 in 4004 BC? (If so, they are "very good".)
- How many dogs were there in the ark? (Were they greyhounds, terriers, poodles, collies …?)

The reason why I consider the matter at all is that I am often asked, as a scientist, how I can believe both scripture and science. Since I find it difficult to restrict God's timing to solar days, I find it even harder to justify a literal reading when it is clouding the main issues of sin, repentance, and forgiveness.

Similarly, we can get hung up on issues such as evolution. Do I believe in evolution? Yes! Do I believe that evolution accounts for life on earth as described by Darwin and others? No, definitely not! We have to assume that Noah had one pair of dogs in the ark. To have had one pair of each breed would have been impossible. The enormous variety of dogs we have today must have evolved from one pair of dogs in the ark—partly by natural interbreeding, partly by human intervention. For dogs to have evolved from some other species is out of the question.

Having faith in a sovereign God who can—and did—create the universe is actually easier than having faith in an unexplainable Big Bang followed by a series of totally random events leading to the amazing beauty and complexity amidst which we have the privilege to live.

There is value in opening such issues up for debate even if we don't agree with them. Some of us have to discuss them outside the hallowed confines of evangelical circles. If we simply shut the door to any discussion without full consideration, then we have very little to support our views when talking to folks who do not accept scripture as evidence. Discussions like this among Christians can be good when we listen to each other and keep calm, seeking to learn from each other. There is the danger, however, that we can create more heat than light and be distracted from our main purposes of worshipping and serving our Creator.

Finally, let us admire Creation but worship only the sovereign Creator. And let us heed the warning of Paul, who said the following of unrighteous people:

> For although they knew God, they did not honour him as God or give thanks to him, but they became futile in their thinking, and their foolish hearts were darkened. Claiming to be wise, they became fools, and exchanged the glory of the immortal God for images resembling mortal man and birds and animals and creeping things. Therefore God gave them up in the lusts of their hearts to impurity, to the dishonouring of their bodies among themselves, because they exchanged the truth about God for a lie and worshipped and served the creature rather than the Creator, who is blessed for ever! Amen. (Romans 1:21–25)

THE SOVEREIGNTY
OF GOD IN LAW

Suggested Background Reading: Exodus 20

Whilst teaching in various places (especially in the science laboratories of various schools and in the education departments in a couple of prisons), I became acutely aware of two different types of law at work. One type is the Law given by God, through Moses, and which is, to a greater or lesser degree, enshrined into the laws enacted by rulers or governments of the nations. This type of law falls into several divisions.

The other type of law is an inherent constituent part of Creation. These laws are those which govern the running of the universe, one of the most obvious of which is the law of gravity. We will have a quick look at this type of law first.

The laws of nature are those which God has instituted for the effective running of His Creation. These are laws which we can observe, we can measure, and we can use to predict certain events. These laws can never be broken, but they can be superseded by a greater law. For example, if I were to hold an object up in the air and then release it, I know that it will start to move towards the centre of the earth, and I can even predict the rate at which it will accelerate as it does so. The law of gravity is universal and is well understood. It can never be broken, though I can prevent the item from falling by not releasing it. This does not break the law, but it does introduce a means by which the law is unable to move the object. The law is still just as active on the object, and I can feel this as I hold the object up, providing a greater effect on it, possibly to the point of finding that my arm starts to ache if I hold it up for too long.

The other type of law is an instruction about what a person should, or should not, do. These laws are rules and regulations which are intended to control our behaviour, rightly or wrongly. The main difference with these laws is that it is possible to disobey them, though there may be consequences resulting from one's disobedience.

Laws of this type may be divided into three categories. We will ignore human laws for now and consider the division of the Mosaic Law into three categories: the moral law, the ceremonial law, and the civil (or judicial) law. This is sometimes referred to as the *tripartite division of the law.*

In the *Second Helvetic Confession* (Chapter XII: The Law of God) we read: "For the sake of clarity we distinguish the moral law which is contained in the Decalogue or two Tables and expounded in the books of Moses, the ceremonial law which determines the ceremonies and worship of God, and the judicial law which is concerned with political and domestic matters."

From the *Westminster Confession of Faith* (Chapter 19: Of the Law of God), we have this:

> II. This law, [the moral law], after his fall, continued to be a perfect rule of righteousness; and, as such, was delivered by God upon Mount Sinai, in ten commandments, and written in two tables: the first four commandments containing our duty towards God; and the other six, our duty to man.

III. Besides this law, commonly called moral, God was pleased to give to the people of Israel, as a church under age, ceremonial laws, containing several typical ordinances, partly of worship, prefiguring Christ, His graces, actions, sufferings, and benefits; and partly, holding forth diverse instructions of moral duties. All which ceremonial laws are now abrogated, under the New Testament.

IV, To them also, as a body politic, He gave sundry judicial laws, which expired together with the State of that people; not obliging under any now, further than the general equity thereof may require.

Tom Schreiner writes the following in his book *40 Questions about Christians and Biblical Law*:

The distinction between the moral, ceremonial, and civil law is appealing and attractive. Even though it has some elements of truth, it does not sufficiently capture Paul's stance toward the law. ... Paul argues that the entirety of the law has been set aside now that Christ has come. To say that the "moral" elements of the law continue to be authoritative blunts the truth that the entire Mosaic covenant is no longer in force for believers. Indeed, it is quite difficult to distinguish between what is "moral" and "ceremonial" in the law. For instance, the law forbidding the taking of interest is clearly a moral mandate.

We read in Exodus 22:25, "If you lend money to any of my people with you who is poor, you shall not be like a money-lender to him, and you shall not exact interest from him."

Clearly, this law was addressed to Israel as an agricultural society in the ancient Near East. As with the rest of the laws in the Mosaic covenant, it is abolished now that Christ has come. This is not to say that this law has nothing to say to the church of Jesus Christ today. It still has a revelatory and pedagogical function.

Still, the distinction has some usefulness, for some of the commands of the law are carried directly over to the New Testament by Paul and applied to the lives of believers. It seems appropriate to designate such commands as moral norms. For instance, the call to honour fathers and mothers still applies to believers.

Ephesians 6:2 reads, "Honour your father and mother." This is the first commandment with a promise.

Paul teaches that love fulfils the law.

> Owe no one anything, except to love each other, for the one who loves another has fulfilled the law. For the commandments, "You shall not commit adultery, You shall not murder, You shall not steal, You shall not covet," and any other commandment, are summed up in this word: "You shall love your neighbour as yourself." Love does no wrong to a neighbour; therefore love is the fulfilling of the law. (Romans 13:8–10)

He clarifies that those who love will not commit adultery, murder, steal, or covet.

> You then who teach others, do you not teach yourself? While you preach against stealing, do you steal? You who say that one must not commit adultery, do you commit adultery? You who abhor idols, do you rob temples? (Romans 2:21–22)

> What then shall we say? That the law is sin? By no means! Yet if it had not been for the law, I would not have known sin. For I would not have known what it is to covet if the law had not said, "You shall not covet." But sin, seizing an

opportunity through the commandment, produced in me
all kinds of covetousness. For apart from the law, sin lies
dead. (Romans 7:7–8)

Those who live according to the Spirit fulfil the requirement of the
Law.

In order that the righteous requirement of the law might
be fulfilled in us, who walk not according to the flesh but
according to the Spirit. (Romans 8:4)

The prohibition against idolatry still stands, though Paul does not
cite the Old Testament law in support.

I wrote to you in my letter not to associate with sexually
immoral people—not at all meaning the sexually immoral
of this world, or the greedy and swindlers, or idolaters,
since then you would need to go out of the world. But now
I am writing to you not to associate with anyone who bears
the name of brother if he is guilty of sexual immorality or
greed, or is an idolater, reviler, drunkard, or swindler—not
even to eat with such a one. (1 Corinthians 5:9–11)

Or do you not know that the unrighteous will not inherit
the kingdom of God? Do not be deceived: neither the
sexually immoral, nor idolaters, nor adulterers, nor men
who practise homosexuality, nor thieves, nor the greedy,
nor drunkards, nor revilers, nor swindlers will inherit the
kingdom of God. (1 Corinthians 6:9–10)

I wish that all were as I myself am. But each has his own
gift from God, one of one kind and one of another. ...
For the unbelieving husband is made holy because of his
wife, and the unbelieving wife is made holy because of her
husband. Otherwise your children would be unclean, but
as it is, they are holy. (1 Corinthians 7:7, 14)

What agreement has the temple of God with idols? For we are the temple of the living God; as God said, "I will make my dwelling among them and walk among them, and I will be their God, and they shall be my people." (2 Corinthians 6:16)

Now the works of the flesh are evident: sexual immorality, impurity, sensuality, idolatry, sorcery, enmity, strife, jealousy, fits of anger, rivalries, dissensions, divisions, envy, drunkenness, orgies, and things like these. I warn you, as I warned you before, that those who do such things will not inherit the kingdom of God. (Galatians 5:19–21)

For you may be sure of this, that everyone who is sexually immoral or impure, or who is covetous (that is, an idolater), has no inheritance in the kingdom of Christ and God. (Ephesians 5:5)

Put to death therefore what is earthly in you: sexual immorality, impurity, passion, evil desire, and covetousness, which is idolatry. (Colossians 3:5)

There are various other commands and prohibitions that reflect the Ten Commandments which are found in Paul's writings.

Question 12. *Are there any situations where the laws of your country conflict with the Law of God? What should you do when this happens?*

The reason why this is such an important topic to discuss is highlighted in the foregoing quotation of Tom Schreiner where he points out that Paul considers the whole of the Old Testament Law to have been fulfilled in the coming of Jesus, yet some parts of that Law are retained as applying to the church, or the whole of society, today.

The ceremonial law is kept by very orthodox Jews only. The judicial law is largely subsumed into secular, civil law today, though its character may be significantly different in many cases. It is the Ten Commandments which many—even most—churches still regard as an integral part of church life and structure. This seems highly illogical.

If we take the Ten Commandments as our rules for living, we must remember that they are all part of one Law. If we break any one of them, we have broken the whole Law. They could be considered to be like a chain on which we are hanging. If we break any one link in the chain, we will fall, even if we have kept the other commandments and all the remaining links in the chain remain intact.

James wrote a very practical letter to a scattered body of people who were suffering hardship and persecution. He made this very point when he wrote that a murderer is not acquitted of murder because he has not committed adultery:

> For whoever keeps the whole law but fails in one point has become accountable for all of it. For he who said, "Do not commit adultery," also said, "Do not murder." If you do not commit adultery but do murder, you have become a transgressor of the law. (James 2:10–11)

Keeping one commandment does not atone for breaking another either. This leaves us with the situation that in order to be right with God, we must be absolutely perfect in the sight of the Law, which is not remotely possible for any of us.

The easiest way to consider the role of the Ten Commandments today is by looking at examples. This has been done to some extent in the preceding discussions, but we can look more closely to see that the Ten Commandments are very much weaker than the One Command which has replaced them.

Laws relating to the offering of sacrifices established that blood had to be shed in order to atone for sin. We read in Leviticus 17:11, "For the life of the flesh is in the blood, and I have given it for you on the altar to make atonement for your souls, for it is the blood that makes atonement by the life."

The use of animals in the Old Testament demonstrates how our sin would be atoned for. Today we accept that Christ was the ultimate sacrifice and we no longer need to use animals, which were only a picture of the Lamb of God.

Much of the other ceremony has also gone from many of our churches, though some have retained the use of robes and candles. The reason for this is obscure.

Question 13. *Do the Ten Commandments apply under the New Covenant as they did under the Old?*

The next big question is "If the ceremonial aspects of the Old Testament Law have been fulfilled in Jesus, then has the moral law been fulfilled in Him also?"

We see that it has been when we turn to the words of Jesus on the subject:

> A new commandment I give to you, that you love one another: just as I have loved you, you also are to love one another. By this all people will know that you are my disciples, if you have love for one another. (John 13:34–35)

We now need to take an example and see how this one new command more than supersedes the ten old ones. The example which is easiest to follow is Exodus 20:15: "You shall not steal." Under the Old Testament Law, this means that we must not take other people's property from them without their permission. Under the New Commandment, we do not show somebody love by stealing from them but by giving to them. This is a much more positive attitude towards other people which more than stops us stealing from them.

This could be applied to each of the Ten Commandments. So, for another example, we can look at the command which forbids coveting. Applying the same principle, not only that we will not covet our neighbour's property but also that we will rejoice with him that he is fortunate enough to own that property.

This brings us to the question about God's sovereignty in law: Why does God allow sin?

The laws of nature which govern the created world were put there by God's sovereign will. These laws cannot be broken unless God chooses to suspend them for a particular purpose. Almost any of the miracles recorded in scripture may serve as an example of this. One specific example would be the floating of an iron axe head when the law of gravity was held back by God in order to resolve a crisis.

> But as one was felling a log, his axe head fell into the water, and he cried out, "Alas, my master! It was borrowed." Then the man of God said, "Where did it fall?" When he showed him the place, he cut off a stick and threw it in there and made the iron float. And he said, "Take it up." So he reached out his hand and took it. (2 Kings 6:5–7)

It is important to note that in every one of the miracles, it is God who alters a law which He made for the orderly running of His Creation and so that the world in which He put us will continue to proceed in a predictable way until He decrees otherwise. This allows for the preservation of life generally and the preservation of His people in particular.

Note that the term "preservation of the saints" is normally used to remind us that a true believer in God is never lost from God's kingdom. This is sometimes rephrased as "Once a Christian, always

85

a Christian." We draw this from the comment by Jesus in His High Priestly Prayer: "I have guarded them, and not one of them has been lost except the son of destruction" (John 17:12).

This is discussed more fully in chapter 10 of *Filtered through Love*.

When considering the other type of law, whether it be moral, ceremonial, or judicial, the situation is very different. It is possible for us to break these laws because God allows us to do so. It would be easy for God in His sovereignty to force us to obey every word of every law, but He has chosen not to do so. We can only speculate as to why this is, because we are not told anywhere in scripture. The real reason may be any one—or any combination—of a number of suggestions such as the following:

We might think that God gives us choice because He wants a people who will be like Him. He gave us many of His attributes when He made us in His own image, including the ability to make choices.

As we read in Genesis 1:27, "So God created man in his own image, in the image of God he created him; male and female he created them."

God wanted to meet with the man whom He had created and to hold conversations with him. God still wants this. There is nothing remotely satisfying about trying to hold a conversation with a robot.

Another suggestion is that God allowed humankind to sin because He wanted to demonstrate His power to overcome sin. There were times in the life of Jesus when this approach was evident. An analogy of this was when He delayed His journey to Bethany until His friend Lazarus had died so that He could show His mastery over death.

> So, when he heard that Lazarus was ill, he stayed two days longer in the place where he was. ...

Then Jesus told them plainly, "Lazarus has died, and for your sake I am glad that I was not there, so that you may believe. But let us go to him." ...

Now when Jesus came, he found that Lazarus had already been in the tomb four days. ... So they took away the stone.

And Jesus lifted up his eyes and said, "Father, I thank you that you have heard me. I knew that you always hear me, but I said this on account of the people standing around, that they may believe that you sent me." When he had said these things, he cried out with a loud voice, "Lazarus, come out." The man who had died came out, his hands and feet bound with linen strips, and his face wrapped with a cloth. Jesus said to them, "Unbind him, and let him go." Many of the Jews therefore, who had come with Mary and had seen what he did, believed in him. (John 11:6, 14–15, 17, 41–45)

It has been suggested that God had ordained that only some of the human race were His elect and, therefore, He had to allow sin into the world as a way of separating them from the others. This does not fit too well with the thinking that a sovereign God could have created a world where only His elect would be. It would, however, avoid the need for any reprobation on God's part. (Reprobation is the sovereign decision of God before Creation to pass over some persons, in sorrow deciding not to save them, and to punish them for their sins.) The support for this suggestion is that God can thereby manifest His justice.

Another idea which has been put forward is that God wanted to make a distinction between good and evil so that he could separate faithful heavenly beings from fallen ones. God cannot bear evil in His presence, so when a heavenly being rebels, God has to cast him out of heaven.

Now war arose in heaven, Michael and his angels fighting against the dragon. And the dragon and his angels fought back, but he was defeated, and there was no longer any place for them in heaven. And the great dragon was thrown down, that ancient serpent, who is called the devil and Satan, the deceiver of the whole world—he was thrown down to the earth, and his angels were thrown down with him. (Revelation 12:7–9)

The final suggestion as to why God allowed humankind to sin is that He was thus able to show His love for us. Without sin there would have been no cross, and without the cross we would not have seen the greatest demonstration of love imaginable as God's sinless Son took our sin upon Himself.

When we think about the sovereignty of God, it is important to remember that one "law" governing God Himself is that He cannot, and will not, betray His own attributes. As a God of love, He cannot tolerate hatred. As a God of truth, He cannot tolerate lies. As a God of holiness and purity, He cannot tolerate evil. This is why He cannot overlook our sin and why He had to send His Son to Calvary to atone for our sin.

What is not possible is that God was taken by surprise when Adam and Eve ate of the forbidden fruit. It is inconceivable that God's plan to send His Son to the cross was an afterthought or a plan B. Nor should we think that the Fall was in any way a sign that God's sovereignty is limited. Just as one of nature's laws cannot be broken but can be subject to another such law, so God's sovereign power—His omnipotence—was subjected to His sovereign will. God deliberately chose to give humankind the ability to obey or not, knowing that we would disobey.

We can be assured that God knew of the Fall before it happened because He knew those of us who were His before He created the earth.

> Blessed be the God and Father of our Lord Jesus Christ, who has blessed us in Christ with every spiritual blessing in the heavenly places, even as he chose us in him before the foundation of the world, that we should be holy and blameless before him. (Ephesians 1:3–4)

When we come to look at the impact of this on our lives, we are reminded of the vast numbers of people living around us who have not come to the point of accepting Christ. We will see later that the fatalistic attitude encouraged by extreme Calvinism is no excuse for failing to reaching out to the lost. Jesus Himself made this clear in the passage which is often called "The Great Commission", which comes with a reminder of the sovereignty of God being expressed in the life of His Son:

> And Jesus came and said to them, "All authority in heaven and on earth has been given to me. Go therefore and make disciples of all nations, baptising them in the name of the Father and of the Son and of the Holy Spirit, teaching them to observe all that I have commanded you. And behold, I am with you always, to the end of the age." (Matthew 28:18–20)

The law for us today is the New Covenant of love. Not only is this the way we have been commanded to live, but also it is the way in which onlookers will recognise us as the people of God. The degree of love required is measured against the standard which Jesus set when He said, "As I have loved you."

We read in John 13:34–35, "A new commandment I give to you, that you love one another: just as I have loved you, you also are to love one another. By this all people will know that you are my disciples, if you have love for one another."

To see what that standard looks like, we need only turn our gaze to the cross. There we see Jesus with His arms stretched as wide as possible as if He saying to us, "I love you *this* much!"

Instead of animal sacrifices, we should be offering prayer as our service of the heart, and also offering our lives, which become a form of living sacrifice. As we lead congregations or other individuals in prayer, we also make those living sacrifices on their behalf, giving them the opportunity to make the prayer their own.

> I appeal to you therefore, brothers, by the mercies of God, to present your bodies as a living sacrifice, holy and acceptable to God, which is your spiritual worship. (Romans 12:1)

> As you come to him, a living stone rejected by men but in the sight of God chosen and precious, you yourselves like living stones are being built up as a spiritual house, to be a holy priesthood, to offer spiritual sacrifices acceptable to God through Jesus Christ. (1 Peter 2:4–5)

> For this very reason, make every effort to supplement your faith with virtue, and virtue with knowledge, and knowledge with self-control, and self-control with steadfastness, and steadfastness with godliness, and godliness with brotherly affection, and brotherly affection with love. For if these qualities are yours and are increasing, they keep you from being ineffective or unfruitful in the knowledge of our Lord Jesus Christ. (2 Peter 1:5–8)

THE SOVEREIGNTY OF GOD IN LEADERSHIP

Suggested Background Reading: Joshua 6

J oshua was a leader who needed to keep control of his military instincts and let God direct his every move. He had already shown himself to be a man who trusted God as he and Caleb were the only two of twelve spies who went into the Promised Land soon after the Israelites left Egypt to encourage the people to go forward in faith.

God punished the unfaithful spies with a plague.

> And the men whom Moses sent to spy out the land, who returned and made all the congregation grumble against him by bringing up a bad report about the land—the men who brought up a bad report of the land—died by plague before the Lord. Of those men who went to spy out the land, only Joshua the son of Nun and Caleb the son of Jephunneh remained alive. (Numbers 14:36–38)

Forty years later, God was ready to take His people into the land He had promised them in the days of Abraham. The first major conquest was to be Jericho, but God had His way of defeating the city. Joshua had to follow God's instructions in detail, and then all was well.

Marching round a city blowing trumpets is not the recognised procedure for taking a city, but it is probably safe to conclude that God had two purposes in this action. Firstly, God wanted to be sure that the people recognised that He was giving Jericho to them without any military skill on their part, and secondly, by so doing, He was showing His people that He could be trusted to keep His covenant concerning the Promised Land.

Joshua 6 has a vivid account of the capture of Jericho. This scripture demonstrates how God can use one man to lead His people, often in unusual ways, to bring His plans to fruition. At the end of the chapter we are told that the city was not to be rebuilt but that the remains would be a reminder of God's power to all who saw them.

In the last few words of the chapter, the writer stresses that there were two other, totally unrelated, outcomes of this event. Firstly, we are told that, as a direct result, the Lord was with Joshua, and secondly we are told that his fame was spread abroad. In the words of Matthew Henry:

> All this magnified Joshua and raised his reputation (Joshua 6:27); it made him not only acceptable to Israel, but formidable to the Canaanites, because it appeared that God was with him of a truth: the Word of the Lord was with him, so the Chaldee, even Christ himself, the same that was with Moses. Nothing can more raise a man's reputation, nor make him appear more truly great, than to have the evidences of God's presence with him.

God's presence with Joshua is evident from the rest of the account of his leadership of God's people. This directs us all to two clear and important lessons, especially if we have responsibility for the leadership of God's people:

Firstly, it is vital that we are sensitive to God leading us as we lead His people on His behalf. God may have ways of doing things which we are not expecting, but we must let Him work out His purposes according to His sovereign plan.

Secondly, we have a responsibility to point those whom we lead to God, in both word and example. Joshua did this with great humility, but very effectively.

> Now therefore fear the Lord and serve him in sincerity and in faithfulness. Put away the gods that your fathers served beyond the River and in Egypt, and serve the Lord. And if it is evil in your eyes to serve the Lord, choose this day whom you will serve, whether the gods your fathers served in the region beyond the River, or the gods of the Amorites in whose land you dwell. But as for me and my house, we will serve the Lord. (Joshua 24:14–15)

The people responded positively, saying they would serve the Lord as they had seen God's faithfulness to Joshua.

Moses was another great leader of the Israelites and probably the more obvious one to choose for a study such as this. God prepared Moses over a period of many years. Moses was born under a sentence of death, his crime being that he was a male Israelite baby in Egypt. Because of his mother's faithfulness, Moses survived, to be brought up in the palace of his condemner, Pharaoh himself. He grew up with a very fiery temper and had to flee from Egypt while he developed patience and humility. So it was when Moses was about eighty years of age that God started to use him as the leader of the Israelites.

The task which God had for Moses was part of His plan which He had described to Abraham, to bring His people into the land He had promised them. The problem was that the people were in slavery in Egypt.

God could have struck the Egyptians down and let His people simply walk free, but according to His purposes, He chose to demonstrate the use of the blood of a lamb in the Israelites' release from captivity in Egypt as a foreshadowing of the blood of His Son, being the means of our release from captivity to sin. He was also intending to demonstrate His power in the sending and removing of the plagues. God chose not to speak to each of the Israelites individually but to speak to one man, whom He appointed as their leader: Moses. This is an important point as it establishes a pattern of leadership which He still uses today.

God told Moses to go to Pharaoh and to take Aaron with him. He gave Moses some signs as evidence of God's involvement. God also warned Moses that Pharaoh would not let the people go at first, but said that they would eventually escape—and plunder the Egyptians when they did so.

> I will stretch out my hand and strike Egypt with all the wonders that I will do in it; after that he will let you go. And I will give this people favour in the sight of the Egyptians; and when you go, you shall not go empty, but each woman shall ask of her neighbour, and any woman who lives in her house, for silver and gold jewellery, and for clothing. You shall put them on your sons and on your daughters. So you shall plunder the Egyptians. (Exodus 3:20–22)

It is also important to notice that the exchanges between Moses and Pharaoh are not a battle of the wills; rather they are totally under the control of God's will. As we read in Exodus 4:21, "But I [God] will harden his [Pharaoh's] heart, so that he will not let the people go.

God had the leader of His people where He wanted him so His sovereign will could be carried out in full. This included the series of ten plagues building up to the death of the firstborn of the Egyptians and the escape of the firstborn of the Israelites, foreshadowing the striking of the Son of God at Calvary.

Throughout their wanderings in the wilderness, God always spoke to His people through Moses, and the people always spoke to God through Moses. The most significant messages that God gave to Moses for the people concerned the way they should live. The Law was centred around the Ten Commandments, but it also gave many instructions about how to worship and how to behave generally. Once again, there were many parts of this which looked forward to the coming of Jesus. This reminds us that God had a plan for His people and was preparing the way for its fulfilment.

God used many unlikely men to lead His people. Gideon was a man with no apparent military or leadership ambitions. We read about him at a time when God was showing the people that their lifestyle had become unacceptable.

As we learn in Judges 6:1, "The people of Israel did what was evil in the sight of the Lord, and the Lord gave them into the hand of Midian for seven years."

When the people turned back to Him in repentance, rather than simply wiping out the Midianites—as He could easily have done—He chose to appoint a leader through whom He would direct the people to remove the Midianites themselves. God chose a man who was timid and in hiding.

> Now the angel of the Lord came and sat under the terebinth
> at Ophrah, which belonged to Joash the Abiezrite, while
> his son Gideon was beating out wheat in the wine press
> to hide it from the Midianites. And the angel of the Lord
> appeared to him and said to him, "The Lord is with you,
> O mighty man of valour." (Judges 6:11–12)

God had to reinforce Gideon's call to leadership by using two very dramatic signs and the instruction to destroy his father's shrine to a false god.

Gideon's first military battle was another example of God's seeming to make things difficult in order to demonstrate that He was the one giving the victory. Gideon had an army of thirty-two thousand men, which God reduced to three hundred before giving the Midian army into his hands. Success came because Gideon led the people according to the instructions God gave him. This is leadership God's way; it achieves God's results and receives God's blessing.

Question 14. *How many of the leaders described in the Bible led the people well, and how many led them astray? Is there a warning for us in this latter fact?*

Samson is a sad case, more an example of how *not* to lead God's people. Samson's mother had been unable to have children until an angel of the Lord told her that God was going to give her a son. We read in Judges 13:7, "Behold, you shall conceive and bear a son. So then drink no wine or strong drink, and eat nothing unclean, for the child shall be a Nazirite to God from the womb to the day of his death."

The father, Manoah, was a man of prayer who was willing to allow his son to be marked out for special service to God and to be under the Nazirite vow. This vow had three main elements:

1. No alcohol was permitted, nor was anything derived from grapes, such as raisins.
2. No contact was permitted with dead bodies of any sort.
3. The hair was not to be cut or trimmed in any way.

There was one hint that things might not go well—Samson's parents were told that Samson would *begin* to save Israel from the hand of the Philistines (Judges 13:5).

At first all seemed to go well as the Lord blessed Samson (Judges 13:24), who was a man of extraordinary strength. This is shown in Judges 14:5–6: "A young lion came towards him roaring. Then the

Spirit of the Lord rushed upon him, and although he had nothing in his hand, he tore the lion in pieces as one tears a young goat."

However, there are three comments made by the writer of Judges which should ring alarm bells. The lion came towards Samson as he was going to meet a woman he wanted to marry.

The first comment had already been made in each of the first three verses of Judges 14 that the woman was a Philistine, one of the invaders. This immediately put Samson outside of God's law forbidding Israelites to marry outside the nation.

The second warning comment was that the lion approached Samson when he was going to meet the woman in a vineyard. This should have been the last place for a Nazirite to be as it violated the first part of the Nazirite vow. It is possible that God sent the lion to warn Samson to keep away from the vineyard and from the Philistine woman.

The third warning comment follows shortly after. When Samson was going to meet the woman again, he passed the carcass of the lion and saw that bees had made use of it. Stealing the honey from the bees may not seem to be a problem, but he had to take the honey from a dead body, thus breaking the second part of his Nazirite vow.

It is remarkable that Samson continued to demonstrate great strength with the help of the Lord. However, when he told Delilah about his Nazirite vow and let her cut his hair, the third part of the vow was lost and his relationship with God suffered as a result.

We read in Judges 16:20, "But he did not know that the Lord had left him."

The man of God had now become a servant of the Midianites—the very people he was supposed to suppress. His strength and sight were both gone, as was his dignity. However, in his death, God gave him strength for one last act against the Philistines, which proved to be the most devastating blow he was to inflict upon them. Samson had gone astray, but God used even this to bring him to the place where He wanted him.

So, even though Samson was far from a model leader, God used him to begin to subdue the Philistines and to achieve His sovereign will.

Question 15. *Do we read of any "perfect" leaders in the Bible apart from Jesus? How does this encourage us?*

Samuel shows us another aspect of good leadership: he had first learned how to be led. We read in 1 Samuel 3:1, "Now the young man Samuel was ministering to the Lord under Eli."

We should also notice that, like Moses, Samuel was brought up in an environment which was an excellent training ground for the task ahead. Whereas Moses grew up in Pharaoh's palace, Samuel spent his formative years in the temple. When the time came for Samuel to lead the people, he already had a very favourable reputation.

> And Samuel grew, and the Lord was with him and let none of his words fall to the ground. And all Israel from Dan to Beersheba knew that Samuel was established as a prophet of the Lord. And the Lord appeared again at Shiloh, for the Lord revealed himself to Samuel at Shiloh by the word of the Lord. (1 Samuel 3:19–21)

Samuel's leadership is a good example for all of us who are leaders. It still speaks to us even if we are not.

> And Samuel said to all the house of Israel, "If you are returning to the Lord with all your heart, then put away the foreign gods and the Ashtaroth from among you and direct your heart to the Lord and serve him only, and he will deliver you out of the hand of the Philistines." So the people of Israel put away the Baals and the Ashtaroth, and

they served the Lord only. Then Samuel said, "Gather all Israel at Mizpah, and I will pray to the Lord for you." (1 Samuel 7:3–5)

The pattern here is that Samuel promised to pray to the Lord, on behalf of the people, for the victory which he had already prophesied would be theirs once they had turned away from the false gods and recommitted themselves to God.

This was typical of Samuel's ministry.

Another important part of Samuel's ministry was the anointing of kings. The first king whom Samuel anointed was Saul. The people had been clamouring for a king "like the other nations" had, which implied that they had rejected God as their King. God had plans in place for this eventuality and had told Samuel of them the day before Saul was to arrive at Zuph, where Samuel was to hold a sacrifice. After spending some time with Saul, Samuel anointed him as had been directed by God. When it came to the formal proclamation of Saul as the newly crowned king, Samuel called the people together. They chose a king by casting lots—even though Saul had already been anointed. Samuel trusted God and knew that the lots would fall on Saul, but the procedure surely made the people feel part of the process, so they would accept Saul as king more easily.

Once more we see that God is firmly in control of events and that Samuel was acting on His leadership.

When God was ready for another king to replace Saul, once again He turned to Samuel. This time He sent him to a specific family, telling Samuel to anoint the least likely member of that family as the next king.

The Lord said to Samuel, "How long will you grieve over Saul, since I have rejected him from being king over Israel? Fill your horn with oil, and go. I will send you to Jesse the

> Bethlehemite, for I have provided for myself a king among his sons." ...
>
> And Jesse made seven of his sons pass before Samuel. And Samuel said to Jesse, "The Lord has not chosen these."
>
> Then Samuel said to Jesse, "Are all your sons here?" And he said, "There remains yet the youngest, but behold, he is keeping the sheep." And Samuel said to Jesse, "Send and get him, for we will not sit down till he comes here." And he sent and brought him in. Now he was ruddy and had beautiful eyes and was handsome. And the Lord said, "Arise, anoint him, for this is he." Then Samuel took the horn of oil and anointed him in the midst of his brothers. And the Spirit of the Lord rushed upon David from that day forward. (1 Samuel 16:1, 10–13)

The important lessons from this are, firstly, that God is in control, leading His leaders; secondly, that earthly leaders should always be sensitive to God's leadership; and thirdly that God sometimes has specific tasks for His leaders to carry out.

It was some considerable time after Samuel anointed David before he became king in Saul's place.

For Samuel, anointing a man to be king was a major responsibility and a privilege. We are unlikely to have such a task to undertake, but we may be called upon to act in a way which may make a large impact on the work of God's kingdom in the lives of either many or just a few.

Nehemiah became a leader not by appointment as such, but by gathering people round him to achieve the goal of rebuilding Jerusalem. One feature of his leadership was the care he took in deciding who would be involved. It would have been easy to welcome anybody to help in the hope of finishing the task more quickly, but some of those present were Samaritans, whom Nehemiah felt would not be fully committed to the task. Ultimately, he refused to allow them to help, which was the beginning of the poor relationship between the Jews and the Samaritans.

Nehemiah 2:20 reads, "Then I replied to them, 'The God of heaven will make us prosper, and we his servants will arise and build, but you have no portion or right or claim in Jerusalem.'" John 4:9 tells us the outcome of this, "For Jews have no dealings with Samaritans."

Nehemiah also showed his leadership skills in the way he used his resources. Chapter 3 of his book tells us how he spread the workers round the city, each with his own section of wall to complete. The skill of Nehemiah's leadership meant that the work proceeded quickly because "the people had a mind to work". Nehemiah never lost sight of the fact that he was working on God's project and with God's help. When opposition came, he knew where to turn. We read in Nehemiah 4:9, "And we prayed to our God and set a guard as a protection against them day and night."

Ezra was a priest who was also a leader of the people during their return from exile and the rebuilding of Jerusalem. With only the walls having been finished, before any houses had been rebuilt, we might have expected housebuilding to be a priority. However, Ezra took his responsibility as a spiritual leader seriously and made sure that the people not only heard the Law of God but also understood it.

> So Ezra the priest brought the Law before the assembly, both men and women and all who could understand what they heard, on the first day of the seventh month. And he read from it facing the square before the Water Gate from early morning until midday, in the presence of the men and the women and those who could understand. And the ears of all the people were attentive to the Book of the Law. … They read from the book, from the Law of God, clearly, and they gave the meaning, so that the people understood the reading. (Nehemiah 8:2–3, 8)

The biblical records of these events do not stress that God was in sovereign control of the work or that He kept giving instructions to Nehemiah and Ezra, but we do know that God had purposed—and promised—that Jerusalem would be rebuilt.

Two hundred years before Jerusalem had even fallen, Amos was warning of the destruction of Israel and of the return of a remnant through whom God would send His Son, Jesus, as our Saviour, thus completing the fulfilment of His covenant promise to Abraham, Isaac, and Jacob.

Amos 9:14 reads, "I will restore the fortunes of my people Israel, and they shall rebuild the ruined cities and inhabit them; they shall plant vineyards and drink their wine, and they shall make gardens and eat their fruit.

Question 16. *Does God always guide His people through a human leader?*

Timothy was the pastor of the church in Ephesus. Paul wrote to him giving advice on leadership in a church situation. This advice still applies in our churches today. It is the same unchangeable sovereign God whose children we are leading, under His direction and in His name.

In his first letter to Timothy, Paul urged him to challenge false teachers and to preach the good news that Christ Jesus had come to save sinners. He stressed the need for prayer not only for those Timothy was leading in the church but also for those in authority under Timothy.

Paul did spell out for Timothy the qualities which leaders in the church should possess. He also encouraged him to lead by example, which included supporting those leaders under him and rewarding those who worked well. Paul then pointed out the need for strength and perseverance.

In the second letter, Paul tells Timothy not to be ashamed of the gospel, saying that he should strive to lead the church well and in a way which would be pleasing to God.

Timothy is also warned of the coming of evil days with Paul saying that he should rely on the authority of scripture as the Word of God and preach it faithfully.

If we have been ordained by God as leaders in His church, we have a high calling indeed. We also have great responsibility because God has put us in a place where He wants us to work towards accomplishing His sovereign purposes.

There are times when we all have to be followers rather than leaders. Paul wrote to the Christians in Rome about submission to the authorities:

> Let every person be subject to the governing authorities. For there is no authority except from God, and those that exist have been instituted by God. Therefore whoever resists the authorities resists what God has appointed, and those who resist will incur judgement. For rulers are not a terror to good conduct, but to bad. Would you have no fear of the one who is in authority? Then do what is good, and you will receive his approval, for he is God's servant for your good. But if you do wrong, be afraid, for he does not bear the sword in vain. For he is the servant of God, an avenger who carries out God's wrath on the wrongdoer. Therefore one must be in subjection, not only to avoid God's wrath but also for the sake of conscience. For because of this you also pay taxes, for the authorities are ministers of God, attending to this very thing. Pay to all what is owed to them: taxes to whom taxes are owed, revenue to whom revenue is owed, respect to whom respect is owed, honour to whom honour is owed. (Romans 13:1–7)

When we are being led, we should be willing to be subject to our leaders. When we are leading, we should do so in such a way which earns their respect and their willingness to follow, but we must also be subject to the leading of God in our lives.

THE SOVEREIGNTY OF GOD IN ADMINISTRATION

Suggested Background Reading: 1 Kings 1–2

There are many occasions in our lives when we make choices about things which may seem to be of little importance or even trivial but which can make a big impact on us at some later time. An example of this is a growing family who needed a larger house. They were also concerned about the local school where their son was about to start. They found an estate near an excellent school with a number of houses on the market. The couple ended up with a choice of about four houses, any of which would have been suitable. After choosing one of the four, they went through the formalities of buying it and moved in. The son was able to start his education at the better school. It was not until later that the couple realised that God had directed them to that particular house. For each of the other houses, the legal process was delayed to the point that they would not have been able to move in for some months. By then it would have been too late to enrol their son in the better school. They would have had to drive him to the other one for a year before moving him away from the friends he would have made there to start again in a strange school.

Another example is even more unexpected. A Christian friend of mine and I were working in a hospital. We went to supper in the staff dining room one evening. We collected our meal and then went to pick up some cutlery before finding a table and sitting down. We bowed our heads for a moment to give thanks for the meal, and when we looked up, there was a nurse standing by our table. Neither of us had seen her before. She told us that she was wanting to meet some Christians and thought that we might be Christians *by the way we picked up our forks!* She said that when we bowed our heads to give thanks her suspicions were confirmed. She proved to be a woman with significant needs for whom Christian fellowship was essential. We were not aware of having picked up our forks in any particular way, but that action was used by God to attract the attention of someone in need.

Throughout scripture we see God at work in matters in which He was preparing for the future or through which He would make some event easier to manage. The same is true of life today, as the foregoing examples demonstrate. We may not realise the sovereignty of God in these matters until later, if ever. Indeed, we may think that we are making the decisions ourselves.

We can see God taking control, behind the scenes, in the transfer of the throne from King David to his son Solomon in the first two chapters of 1 Kings.

David had many sons. The oldest was Amnon, killed by his half-brother Absalom for the rape of their sister Tamar.

The second son, known as Chileab (2 Samuel 3:3) or Daniel (1 Chronicles 3:1), is otherwise unknown.

Absalom, the third son, was himself killed by Joab, one of David's military leaders, hoping (wrongly) to win the approval of David for doing so.

The fourth son of David was Adonijah. When David was nearing the end of his life, Adonijah attempted to become king in David's place. If Daniel (Chileab) had died, then Adonijah may have thought that the throne was rightfully his, but God had other plans. In any case, Adonijah was wrong to have exalted himself (1 Kings 1:5) and also for not having waited until David had died. An intervention by Nathan the prophet and Bathsheba, Solomon's mother, led David to make Solomon king. Adonijah was soon put to death.

This outcome, clearly stated in the last sentence of 1 Kings 2—"So the kingdom was established in the hand of Solomon"—was clearly in line with God's sovereign will.

> David said to Solomon, "My son, I had it in my heart to build a house to the name of the Lord my God. But the word of the Lord came to me, saying, 'You have shed much blood and have waged great wars. You shall not build a house to my name, because you have shed so much blood before me on the earth. Behold, a son shall be born to you who shall be a man of rest. I will give him rest from all his surrounding enemies. For his name shall be Solomon, and I will give peace and quiet to Israel in his days. He shall build a house for my name. He shall be my son, and I will be his father, and I will establish his royal throne in Israel forever.'" (1 Chronicles 22:7–10)

Solomon also experienced God's wisdom in the administration of the building of the Temple. Soon after we read about Solomon becoming king, we have an account of the details of how the Temple should be built, as follows:

> And the Lord gave Solomon wisdom, as he promised him. And there was peace between Hiram and Solomon, and the two of them made a treaty.
>
> King Solomon drafted forced labour out of all Israel, and the draft numbered 30,000 men. And he sent them to Lebanon, 10,000 a month in shifts. They would be a month in Lebanon and two months at home. Adoniram was in

charge of the draft. Solomon also had 70,000 burden-bearers and 80,000 stonecutters in the hill country, besides Solomon's 3,300 chief officers who were over the work, who had charge of the people who carried on the work. (1 Kings 5:12–16)

Although we are not told that God gave specifications for the Temple building, it is clear that God was taking a close interest in the work.

> Now the word of the Lord came to Solomon, "Concerning this house that you are building, if you will walk in my statutes and obey my rules and keep all my commandments and walk in them, then I will establish my word with you, which I spoke to David your father. And I will dwell among the children of Israel and will not forsake my people Israel." (1 Kings 6:11–13)

The Temple was costly, but God had ordained that the Temple would be a place where He would be glorified and would be with His people. The same is true today, but now the "Temple", also costly (the cost having been paid at Calvary), is the body of the believer, where God should be glorified. As we read in 1 Corinthians 6:19–20, "Or do you not know that your body is a temple of the Holy Spirit within you, whom you have from God? You are not your own, for you were bought with a price. So glorify God in your body."

For Noah building the ark, the task must have been just as challenging. The ark was a much simpler structure than the Temple, but building methods were relatively primitive. In this case, though, God gave specific details of its construction design and size:

> Make yourself an ark of gopher wood. Make rooms in the ark, and cover it inside and out with pitch. This is how you are to make it: the length of the ark 300 cubits, its breadth 50 cubits, and its height 30 cubits. Make a roof for the ark, and finish it to a cubit above, and set the door of the ark

in its side. Make it with lower, second, and third decks. (Genesis 6:14–16)

The surrounding narrative tells us that God had purposed to destroy the earth by flooding, but He had already indicated that a descendant of Adam and Eve would bring redemption (this is sometimes called the "protogospel").

We read in Genesis 3:15, "I will put enmity between you and the woman, and between your offspring and her offspring; he shall bruise your head, and you shall bruise his heel." God had to keep this promise by not destroying every human being on the earth, but saving some to continue the family of Adam and Eve, at least as far as the coming of Jesus as our Redeemer.

The fact that evil had grown between the time of the Fall and the time of Noah was not a surprise to God. He had always planned to destroy evil and save those who were faithful to Him in Noah's time, just as He has been doing throughout the whole of human history.

Noah was enclosed in the ark for a time, and as a result his family was saved from destruction. Jesus was enclosed in the tomb for a time, and as a result His church is being saved from eternal destruction. God included the Flood in His sovereign plans in order to demonstrate His way of salvation. His plans, fully detailed, demonstrated His understanding of the needs of the creatures He had created.

Question 17. *How does God guide us in the decisions we make?*

When we turn our attention to the Exodus from Egypt, we see another amazing example of God putting His plans into action to prepare for the fulfilment of His purposes many years later.

God set forth a strict set of procedures which His people were to follow on that final night in Goshen. Exodus 12 gives the details of the sacrifice of a perfect lamb, when and where this should be done, how the blood should be displayed on the doorposts, the fact that the meal should include unleavened bread, and how the people were to be dressed. Unleavened bread was used because it is the quickest to bake—and the people were to leave in a hurry. And yeast (leaven) in scripture speaks of sin.

Once again, God was directing these events to demonstrate His plans for His church. The Israelites were brought out of slavery in Egypt, having been saved by the shed blood of a perfect lamb. God's New Covenant people—the church—are brought out of slavery to sin by the shed blood of the perfect Lamb of God.

God did not leave it at that. He instituted the Passover memorial feast, which also involves unleavened bread and wine, as a token of the shed blood of the lamb. Details of this are also found in the same chapter of Exodus. Whilst this was given to the Israelites as a way of remembering what God did for them on that Passover night, as we saw earlier, in chapter 2, Jesus changed its meaning and gave it to us as a memorial of His death at Calvary.

> And he took a cup, and when he had given thanks he said, "Take this, and divide it among yourselves. For I tell you that from now on I will not drink of the fruit of the vine until the kingdom of God comes." And he took bread, and when he had given thanks, he broke it and gave it to them, saying, "This is my body, which is given for you. Do this in remembrance of me." And likewise the cup after they had eaten, saying, "This cup that is poured out for you is the new covenant in my blood." (Luke 22:17–20)

The first cup here is the Passover cup, which Jesus took again (v. 20) to represent His own blood. In verse 18, Jesus also points us forward to His Second Coming, when we will drink with Him in God's glorious kingdom.

As the Israelites wandered through the wilderness, God gave them instructions for the building of the tabernacle and the Ark of the Covenant.

Once more, the detailed designs were given by God, and these were followed precisely as they were full of symbolism. The Ark was to represent the presence of God with His people, whereas the tabernacle was to represent the place where God would come to speak to them.

> Exactly as I show you concerning the pattern of the tabernacle, and of all its furniture, so you shall make it. They shall make an ark of acacia wood. Two cubits and a half shall be its length, a cubit and a half its breadth, and a cubit and a half its height. You shall overlay it with pure gold, inside and outside shall you overlay it, and you shall make on it a moulding of gold round it. You shall cast four rings of gold for it and put them on its four feet, two rings on one side of it, and two rings on the other side of it. You shall make poles of acacia wood and overlay them with gold. And you shall put the poles into the rings on the sides of the ark to carry the ark by them. The poles shall remain in the rings of the ark; they shall not be taken from it. And you shall put into the ark the testimony that I shall give you. (Exodus 25:9–16)

These details are not important for us in this context. The record is given in scripture so that we may imagine and marvel at the beauty of the Ark, and also see that God gave the details to Moses so that the Ark would be appropriate for its purpose.

Elsewhere in the Law which God gave through Moses, there are many demonstrations of the way in which He intervened in the administration of daily life of the early Israelite nation. These demonstrations show that the sovereign God had the welfare of His people at heart and that He wanted them to live in fellowship with Him.

Two groups of the population were particularly vulnerable in Old Testament times. These were children who were orphaned before being able to fend for themselves, and widows.

We read of orphans being taken under the wings of older relatives, an example of which is Esther, who was brought up by her older cousin.

> Now there was a Jew in Susa the citadel whose name was Mordecai, the son of Jair, son of Shimei, son of Kish, a Benjaminite, who had been carried away from Jerusalem among the captives carried away with Jeconiah king of Judah, whom Nebuchadnezzar king of Babylon had carried away. He was bringing up Hadassah, that is Esther, the daughter of his uncle, for she had neither father nor mother. The young woman had a beautiful figure and was lovely to look at, and when her father and her mother died, Mordecai took her as his own daughter. (Esther 2:5–7)

God put measures in place to support those who were not cared for in this way. In the book of Leviticus we are told of God's provision of food for those in need by allowing them to glean after the reapers at harvest time. Farmers were not permitted to harvest right into the corners of their fields, and any of the harvest which was left in the fields was not to be collected. To wit, Leviticus 23:22: "And when you reap the harvest of your land, you shall not reap your field right up to its edge, nor shall you gather the gleanings after your harvest. You shall leave them for the poor and for the sojourner: I am the Lord your God."

Earlier in the same book, we read that God had already given these instructions with various other measures to avoid the exploitation of the poor and vulnerable:

> When you reap the harvest of your land, you shall not reap your field right up to its edge, neither shall you gather the gleanings after your harvest. And you shall not strip your

vineyard bare, neither shall you gather the fallen grapes of your vineyard. You shall leave them for the poor and for the sojourner: I am the Lord your God.

You shall not steal; you shall not deal falsely; you shall not lie to one another. You shall not swear by my name falsely, and so profane the name of your God: I am the Lord.

You shall not oppress your neighbour or rob him. The wages of a hired servant shall not remain with you all night until the morning. You shall not curse the deaf or put a stumbling block before the blind, but you shall fear your God: I am the Lord.

You shall do no injustice in court. You shall not be partial to the poor or defer to the great, but in righteousness shall you judge your neighbour. You shall not go around as a slanderer among your people, and you shall not stand up against the life of your neighbour: I am the Lord.

You shall not hate your brother in your heart, but you shall reason frankly with your neighbour, lest you incur sin because of him. You shall not take vengeance or bear a grudge against the sons of your own people, but you shall love your neighbour as yourself: I am the Lord. (Leviticus 19:9–18)

We are reminded of God's sovereignty by the phrase "I am the Lord" after each instruction.

Much of this is centred around the theme of the Ten Commandments and the call to love one another. As we read this, we may be reminded of the words of Jesus we noted in chapter 6 where He gives us a statement of the measure of love expected and points out that our love for each other will shine out to the world around us. As we read in John 13:34–35, "A new commandment I give to you, that you love one another: just as I have loved you, you also are to love one another.

By this all people will know that you are my disciples, if you have love for one another."

The year of jubilee was instituted by God to stop wealthy folk from exploiting the vulnerable by buying their land and driving them into poverty so that they would not be able to sustain themselves. The year of jubilee meant that land was effectively sold leasehold and would be returned to its former owner in the jubilee year.

> And you shall consecrate the fiftieth year, and proclaim liberty throughout the land to all its inhabitants. It shall be a jubilee for you, when each of you shall return to his property and each of you shall return to his clan. That fiftieth year shall be a jubilee for you; in it you shall neither sow nor reap what grows of itself nor gather the grapes from the undressed vines. For it is a jubilee. It shall be holy to you. (Leviticus 25:10–12)

A similar arrangement was also included in the Law to apply to land at times other than jubilee years and also to other property, including slaves. Leviticus 25 gives details about how redemption of property was to be administered. There are provisions for property to be redeemed by a near kinsman, or "goel".

We read in Leviticus 25:25, "If your brother becomes poor and sells part of his property, then his nearest redeemer shall come and redeem what his brother has sold." The chapter ends with a phrase which we met before where God reminds the people of His sovereign right to demand these things, saying, "I am the Lord your God."

Part of God's plan for His people was that business was to be conducted in a fair and honest way.

> You shall not have in your bag two kinds of weights, a large and a small. You shall not have in your house two kinds of measures, a large and a small. A full and fair weight you shall have, a full and fair measure you shall have, that your days may be long in the land that the Lord your God is giving you. For all who do such things, all who act dishonestly, are an abomination to the Lord your God. (Deuteronomy 25:13–16)

The administration of legacies was equally important in God's sight. If a man were to die, his sons would automatically inherit his estate, but God ensured that in unusual cases there would be no squabbling. Instead, the transfer of the estate would be handled in a calm and dignified way.

> If a man dies and has no son, then you shall transfer his inheritance to his daughter. And if he has no daughter, then you shall give his inheritance to his brothers. And if he has no brothers, then you shall give his inheritance to his father's brothers. And if his father has no brothers, then you shall give his inheritance to the nearest kinsman of his clan, and he shall possess it. (Numbers 27:8–11)

A provision which God made for widows is similar in some ways to the goel and is sometimes confused with it. This is "levirate marriage":

> If brothers dwell together, and one of them dies and has no son, the wife of the dead man shall not be married outside the family to a stranger. Her husband's brother shall go in to her and take her as his wife and perform the duty of a husband's brother to her. And the first son whom she bears shall succeed to the name of his dead brother, that his name may not be blotted out of Israel. (Deuteronomy 25:5–6)

The story of Ruth is one where the goel and the levirate come together. The unnamed near-kinsman was willing to redeem the land which

Elimelech had sold before he took his family to Moab, but he was not willing to marry Ruth as a levirate because then their son would have been, in effect, Mahlon's son, not his own. He was afraid that this would compromise his own estate's future. Boaz stepped in and married Ruth—it seems for love rather than formal levirate responsibilities—and also redeemed Elimelech's land. Not only did Boaz take care of Ruth, but also he looked after Naomi. We should also notice that the man who failed to marry Ruth for risk of losing his name is the one key player whose name is not recorded here!

These arrangements are not just there to keep the peace and stop arguments. They stem from a real concern which God has for His people.

There would have been many pressures on a widow in Old Testament times, just as there are in many parts of the world today. A widow who was not able to remarry or to be taken in by a friend could only look forward to a life of poverty, relying on gleaning or begging for food, or else she would earn money by prostituting herself or by selling herself into slavery. Then she would be easy prey for rapists and other types of abusers.

Question 18. *Are the choices we make without thinking important to God?*

The purity of the Jewish nation was of great importance to God as it was to demonstrate the intended purity of the Christian church. God said of the former inhabitants of the land:

> Nor shall you make marriages with them. You shall not give your daughter to their son, nor take their daughter for your son. For they will turn your sons away from following Me, to serve other gods; so the anger of the Lord will be aroused against you and destroy you suddenly. (Deuteronomy 7:3–4)

This is one of a number of times when God forbade the Jews to marry Gentiles. In another He gives the reason:

> Take heed to yourself, lest you make a covenant with the inhabitants of the land where you are going, lest it be a snare in your midst ... and you take of his daughters for your sons, and his daughters play the harlot with their gods and make your sons play the harlot with their gods. (Exodus 34:12, 16)

He raises the issue again, through Joshua:

> Therefore take careful heed to yourselves, that you love the Lord your God. Or else, if indeed you do go back, and cling to the remnant of these nations—these that remain among you—and make marriages with them, and go in to them and they to you, know for certain that the Lord your God will no longer drive out these nations from before you. But they shall be snares and traps to you, and scourges on your sides and thorns in your eyes, until you perish from this good land which the Lord your God has given you. (Joshua 23:11–13)

Nehemiah pleads with the people on the same subject and points out that even Solomon's life could have ended in disaster as a result of marriages outside the Jewish nation.

> Did not Solomon king of Israel sin by these things? Yet among many nations there was no king like him, who was beloved of his God; and God made him king over all Israel. Nevertheless pagan women caused even him to sin. Should we then hear of your doing all this great evil, transgressing against our God by marrying pagan women? (Nehemiah 13:26–27)

Arguably the most direct display of God's sovereignty is when He administered the three main feasts (*moadim*) for the Israelites as they wandered in the wilderness in preparation for entering the Promised Land.

> Three times in the year you shall keep a feast to me. You shall keep the Feast of Unleavened Bread. As I commanded you, you shall eat unleavened bread for seven days at the appointed time in the month of Abib, for in it you came out of Egypt. None shall appear before me empty-handed. You shall keep the Feast of Harvest, of the firstfruits of your labour, of what you sow in the field. You shall keep the Feast of Ingathering at the end of the year, when you gather in from the field the fruit of your labour. Three times in the year shall all your males appear before the Lord God. (Exodus 23:14–17)

The first significant point is that all male Jews were to appear before the Lord. They were told later that this was to be in Jerusalem.

The first feast was the Feast of Unleavened Bread, also known as the Passover. More precisely, the Feast of Unleavened Bread lasted for a week, with the Passover Feast as its climax. The timing of this was fixed as the anniversary of the Exodus.

The second feast, the Feast of Harvest, was also to be at a fixed time— seven weeks and one day after the Passover. As a result, it became known as the Feast of Weeks and later as Pentecost. This represented the *beginning* of harvest.

The third feast, known variously as the Feast of Tabernacles or the Feast of Booths, marked the end of harvest and was rather more open-ended as to when it took place.

All this shows that God was in control and planning for the ministry of His Son on earth. The population of Jerusalem would be several times its normal size while these feasts were happening.

Jesus rode into Jerusalem at the beginning of the Feast of Unleavened Bread, a time when there would have been the maximum number of people there to wave palm branches and shout "Hosanna." By the end of the week there would still have been the maximum number of people there to witness His crucifixion. We have already seen the relationship between the Exodus from slavery in Egypt and the freedom from the bondage of sin for the believer.

Fifty days later, Jerusalem would, again, have been host to the maximum number of people, so many would have been there to witness the coming of the Holy Spirit at Pentecost. If this feast used to represent the beginning of the harvest, then we can safely link it to represent the harvest of souls which is the church.

Using this picture, we could take the third feast—at a time we have not been told—to mean the end of the harvest of souls, the end of time, and the return of Jesus in triumph and glory. As we read in Revelation 1:7, "Behold, he is coming with the clouds, and every eye will see him, even those who pierced him, and all tribes of the earth will wail on account of him. Even so. Amen."

THE SOVEREIGNTY OF GOD IN SPIRITUALITY

Suggested Background Reading: Amos 5

Amos was an unlikely chap to be a prophet. He began as a shepherd in Tekoa, a lonely village in Judah, a few miles south of Bethlehem. The majority of his prophecy was directed towards Israel, a few years before Samaria fell to the Syrians. The Israelites had enjoyed a lengthy time of peace and had become quite wealthy. There were many trade routes through the land, and taxation had been welcome. However, it was the rich who had become wealthy, while the poor became oppressed and suffered at the hands of their own people. The rich loaned money to the poor at extortionate rates of interest, and bribery and corruption were rife, as we see in Amos 5:12: "For I know how many are your transgressions and how great are your sins—you who afflict the righteous, who take a bribe, and turn aside the needy in the gate."

Throughout chapter 5 of Amos's prophecy, we see him appealing to the Israelites. However, the thrust of the message—in this chapter at least—is not aimed primarily at specific evils, but at the spiritual state of the people and their attitude towards God. Amos reminds the people of the greatness and the sovereignty of God in Creation:

"He who made the Pleiades and Orion, and turns deep darkness into the morning and darkens the day into night, who calls for the waters of the sea and pours them out on the surface of the earth, the Lord is his name." (Amos 5:8)

Later, Amos talks of "the Lord, the God of Hosts", drawing attention to God's military sovereignty, before calling on Israel to turn towards good and away from evil so that the same sovereign God would be with them, being gracious to them. "Seek good, and not evil, that you may live; and so the Lord, the God of hosts, will be with you, as you have said. Hate evil, and love good, and establish justice in the gate; it may be that the Lord, the God of hosts, will be gracious to the remnant of Joseph." (Amos 5:14)

The fact that Amos refers to "those who are skilled in lamentation" suggests that he is talking about some very serious trouble ahead, but if the Lord was going to "pass through their midst", they would not have been able to hide their evil, or hide themselves, as Adam tried to hide himself in the Garden of Eden.

"'They shall call the farmers to mourning and to wailing those who are skilled in lamentation, and in all vineyards there shall be wailing, for I will pass through your midst,' says the Lord." (Amos 5:16-17)

Amos was warning the Israelites of the consequences of their lack of spirituality. The fact that the warnings were not heeded and that God did take the action He said—and that the Israelites were taken into captivity—demonstrates once more that He is the sovereign God who can, and does, discipline those whom He loves. "'And I will send you into exile beyond Damascus,' says the Lord, whose name is the God of hosts." (Amos 5:27)

The Assyrians came from beyond Damascus and took the people of the northern kingdom of Israel into captivity in, or about, the year 722 BC. The southern kingdom of Judah, failing to learn the lesson of this, saw Jerusalem fall to the Babylonians some one hundred thirty-six years later.

We should make two points in particular here:

Firstly, it is clear that God was requiring the Israelites to follow the way of righteousness, rather than punishing them in revenge. As we read in Amos 5:24, "But let justice roll down like waters, and righteousness like an ever-flowing stream."

Secondly, the whole of the last part of Amos 5 (the last ten verses or so) shows that God was looking for sincerity of heart, and He would not accept ritual formalities such as sacrifices and offerings which were not genuine worship.

One of the early inhabitants of the earth was Enoch. When we read of him in his place in history, we are told simply that he walked with God and that God took him, apparently without his experiencing death.

> When Enoch had lived for 65 years, he fathered Methuselah. Enoch walked with God after he fathered Methuselah for 300 years and had other sons and daughters. Thus all the days of Enoch were 365 years. Enoch walked with God, and he was not, for God took him. (Genesis 5:21–24)

When we turn to the letter to the Hebrews, we find that Enoch did, indeed, escape death. The writer to the Hebrews puts this into the context of the faith Enoch had in God:

> By faith Enoch was taken up so that he should not see death, and he was not found, because God had taken him. Now before he was taken, he was commended as having pleased God. And without faith it is impossible to please him, for whoever would draw near to God must believe that he exists and that he rewards those who seek him. (Hebrews 11:5–6)

Enoch had a spirituality and a faith which was pleasing to God. When we think of God as punishing sin, which we do often, especially as we read the Old Testament prophecies, we are in danger of overlooking the promise that God rewards those who come to Him in faith and spiritual worship.

In his general letter, Jude discussed false teachers and those who are spiritually barren. Jude 1:10 reads, "But these people blaspheme all that they do not understand, and they are destroyed by all that they, like unreasoning animals, understand instinctively."

While Jude is thinking about those with no spiritual insight, he refers to Enoch by way of contrast, and he quotes him as a prophet:

> It was also about these that Enoch, the seventh from Adam, prophesied, saying, "Behold, the Lord comes with ten thousands of his holy ones, to execute judgement on all and to convict all the ungodly of all their deeds of ungodliness that they have committed in such an ungodly way, and of all the harsh things that ungodly sinners have spoken against him." (Jude 14–15)

Question 19. *Jude recognised Enoch as a prophet by his spirituality. Does this way of recognising God's people still work today?*

The message of Enoch as it applies to us is found in Paul's letter to the Christians in Rome: "I appeal to you therefore, brothers, by the mercies of God, to present your bodies as a living sacrifice, holy and acceptable to God, which is your spiritual worship" (Romans 12:1). This is how we can let God fulfil His purposes in us and through us to His honour and glory.

It is encouraging to see men in scripture who have a true relationship with God yet have flawed characters. I find this encouraging not because we can sin deliberately and get away with it but because we see that our sin does not mean that God gives up on us.

David had a spiritual relationship with God before and after his committing adultery with Bathsheba.

In his early days, David stood in contrast to Saul, but God brought them together so David would learn something of life as a king.

> Now the Spirit of the Lord departed from Saul, and a harmful spirit from the Lord tormented him. ... And whenever the harmful spirit from God was upon Saul, David took the lyre and played it with his hand. So Saul was refreshed and was well, and the harmful spirit departed from him. (1 Samuel 16:14, 23)

God's action was more than withdrawing His Spirit from Saul. He also sent Saul a harmful spirit as a step towards preparing the way for David to become king.

> The next day a harmful spirit from God rushed upon Saul, and he raved within his house while David was playing the lyre, as he did day by day. Saul had his spear in his hand. And Saul hurled the spear, for he thought, "I will pin David to the wall." But David evaded him twice. ... But when Saul saw and knew that the Lord was with David, and that Michal, Saul's daughter, loved him, Saul was even more afraid of David. (1 Samuel 18:10–11, 28-29)

Saul's subsequent pursuit of David was ordained by the sovereign God as yet another part of David's preparation for his forthcoming responsibilities, so that David could demonstrate his patience and his faith in God. These dark days for David may be seen as God working out His sovereignty in the spirituality of David.

In the later life of David, we see both his spirituality and his acknowledgement of the sovereignty of God expressed poetically in many of the psalms. In Psalm 3, for example, David describes fleeing from the treachery of his son Absalom, and speaks not of the danger of Absalom but of the protection of the Lord. The psalm shows that David had a spiritual relationship with God and that he acknowledged God's sovereignty in salvation.

> But you, O Lord, are a shield about me,
> my glory, and the lifter of my head.
> I cried aloud to the Lord,
> and he answered me from his holy hill. ...
> Salvation belongs to the Lord;
> your blessing be on your people! (Psalm 3:3–4, 8)

Psalm 4 has a similar theme as a prayer to God, but David also calls on his earthly hearers to turn to God:

> Offer right sacrifices,
> and put your trust in the Lord.
> There are many who say, "Who will show us some good?
> Lift up the light of your face upon us, O Lord!" (Psalm 4:5–6)

Psalm 6 is another prayer in which David expresses his confidence in the power of God to defeat his enemies:

> All my enemies shall be ashamed and greatly troubled;
> they shall turn back and be put to shame in a moment.
> (Psalm 6:10)

In Psalm 8, David is again praising the greatness and majesty of God and standing in awe of Him:

> O Lord, our Lord,
> how majestic is your name in all the earth!
> You have set your glory above the heavens. ...
> What is man that you are mindful of him,
> and the son of man that you care for him?...
> O Lord, our Lord,
> how majestic is your name in all the earth! (Psalm 8:1, 4, 9)

Psalm 9 is another which focuses on God's sovereignty:

> When my enemies turn back,
> they stumble and perish before your presence. ...
> But the Lord sits enthroned for ever;
> he has established his throne for justice. (Psalm 9:3, 7)

Psalm 51 is a powerful expression of David's remorse at having committed adultery with Bathsheba. Even though the relationship between David and God had been seriously strained, God had not forsaken David. He had plans for David which He was yet to fulfil.

> Have mercy on me, O God,
> according to your steadfast love;
> according to your abundant mercy
> blot out my transgressions.
> Wash me thoroughly from my iniquity,
> and cleanse me from my sin! ...
> The sacrifices of God are a broken spirit;
> a broken and contrite heart, O God, you will not despise.
> (Psalm 51:1, 2, 17)

David came to this point of repentance because God, in His sovereignty and His love, sent Nathan to him to restore David spiritually by pointing out the sin in his life, not only in the adultery with Bathsheba but also in causing her husband, Uriah, to be killed in battle. (The details of this may be found in 2 Samuel 11–12.)

The writer of the Chronicles records for us that David organised the musicians for the worship of God. Among them was a man named Jeduthun.

> David and the chiefs of the service also set apart for the
> service the sons of Asaph, and of Heman, and of Jeduthun,
> whoprophesiedwithlyres, with harps, andwithcymbals....
> Jeduthun, the sons of Jeduthun: Gedaliah, Zeri, Jeshaiah,

> Shimei, Hashabiah, and Mattithiah, six, under the direction
> of their father Jeduthun, who prophesied with the lyre in
> thanksgiving and praise to the Lord. (1 Chronicles 25:1, 3)

Jeduthun, therefore, was a man involved with the worship of God, so he was central to the spiritual well-being of the nation. So, it was to Jeduthun that David addressed some of his psalms. Psalm 39, for example, is a prayer of David in which he acknowledges the sovereignty of God over his own life, while confessing the frailty of human life generally and his own mortality in particular.

> O Lord, make me know my end
> and what is the measure of my days;
> let me know how fleeting I am!
> Behold, you have made my days a few handbreadths,
> and my lifetime is as nothing before you.
> Surely all mankind stands as a mere breath! …
> Hear my prayer, O Lord,
> and give ear to my cry. (Psalm 39:4, 5, 12)

Psalm 62 is another which David wrote for Jeduthun to sing. Once more the sovereignty of God is affirmed ("power belongs to God") in the context of praise ("He is my rock") and meditation ("wait in silence"):

> For God alone, O my soul, wait in silence,
> for my hope is from him.
> He only is my rock and my salvation,
> my fortress; I shall not be shaken.
> On God rests my salvation and my glory;
> my mighty rock, my refuge is God.
> Trust in him at all times, O people;
> pour out your heart before him;
> God is a refuge for us. …
> Once God has spoken;
> twice have I heard this:
> that power belongs to God,

and that to you, O Lord, belongs steadfast love.
For you will render to a man
according to his work. (Psalm 62:5–8, 11–12)

In the best-known of all the psalms, Psalm 23, David is rejoicing in his spiritual relationship with God whilst also expressing his confidence in the ability of the sovereign God to protect him for the rest of his life and in eternity: "Surely goodness and mercy shall follow me all the days of my life, and I shall dwell in the house of the Lord for ever" (Psalm 23:6).

In all these psalms and many others, we see that God's sovereignty is evident when David is in a good spiritual relationship with God. This does not mean that God was not sovereign when David's relationship with God was not right, but it indicates that when David was "in tune" with God, he was more acutely aware of His sovereignty.

We should also see that when David spoiled his relationship with God by engaging in adultery, God sent Nathan to draw him gently back. Never do we read of God forcing David into spirituality. Had He done so, then the worship would have been unlikely to be genuine and acceptable to God.

Question 20. *Given that Amos preached against the general lack of spirituality among God's people, rather than against specific evils, how should following this example affect us and our ministry?*

In the book of Daniel we have examples of God demonstrating His sovereignty by intervening in the natural world in situations where His people were standing up for their faith in God in the face of opposition from the pagan world around them. Daniel and his friends had been taken into captivity in Babylon. They were chosen as potential servants in the king's palace and were expected to eat food which they thought would have been offered to idols. Daniel realised that spirituality was more important than eating luxury food, so he refused to eat the food. Despite living on inferior rations, Daniel and his friends were in better condition after a few days than those who ate the best food.

God showed that he honoured those who stood up for what was right by giving them favour in the sight of their masters and by altering the processes of human development—processes which He had created in the first place—within a very short time.

> But Daniel resolved that he would not defile himself with the king's food, or with the wine that he drank. Therefore, he asked the chief of the eunuchs to allow him not to defile himself. And God gave Daniel favour and compassion in the sight of the chief of the eunuchs. ... So he listened to them in this matter, and tested them for ten days. At the end of ten days it was seen that they were better in appearance and fatter in flesh than all the youths who ate the king's food. (Daniel 1:8–9, 14–15)

A more dramatic account of God's sovereignty over His creation is found a little later in the book of Daniel. Here, again, God's action is in response to the spirituality of His people in refusing to bow down to a false god—the image set up by Nebuchadnezzar. They also had stood up to malicious accusations by some of the Chaldeans who were trying to make as much trouble as possible for the Jews.

> And the herald proclaimed aloud, "You are commanded, O peoples, nations, and languages, that when you hear the sound of the horn, pipe, lyre, trigon, harp, bagpipe, and every kind of music, you are to fall down and worship the golden image that King Nebuchadnezzar has set up. And whoever does not fall down and worship shall immediately be cast into a burning fiery furnace." ... Therefore at that time certain Chaldeans came forward and maliciously accused the Jews. ... And he ordered some of the mighty men of his army to bind Shadrach, Meshach, and Abednego, and to cast them into the burning fiery furnace. Then these men were bound in their cloaks, their tunics, their hats, and their other garments, and they were thrown into the burning fiery furnace. Because the king's

order was urgent and the furnace overheated, the flame of the fire killed those men who took up Shadrach, Meshach, and Abednego. And these three men, Shadrach, Meshach, and Abednego, fell bound into the burning fiery furnace. Then King Nebuchadnezzar was astonished and rose up in haste. He declared to his counsellors, "Did we not cast three men bound into the fire?" They answered and said to the king, "True, O king." He answered and said, "But I see four men unbound, walking in the midst of the fire, and they are not hurt; and the appearance of the fourth is like a son of the gods." (Daniel 3:4–6, 8, 20–25)

Another well-known incident in the life of Daniel concerns the den of lions. Daniel's life reflected his spirituality and he found favour with the king. As a result, the king gave him responsibilities in the running of the kingdom, but this aroused the jealousy of native Chaldeans. They devised a plot to undermine Daniel's spirituality, but they failed to take God's sovereignty into account. Once more, God showed His mastery over nature by not letting hungry lions touch Daniel, whereas when Daniel's accusers were thrown into the pit, the lions tore them to pieces before they even had reached the bottom of the pit.

Then this Daniel became distinguished above all the other presidents and satraps, because an excellent spirit was in him. And the king planned to set him over the whole kingdom. ... All the presidents of the kingdom, the prefects and the satraps, the counsellors and the governors are agreed that the king should establish an ordinance and enforce an injunction, that whoever makes petition to any god or man for thirty days, except to you, O king, shall be cast into the den of lions. ... When Daniel knew that the document had been signed, he went to his house where he had windows in his upper chamber open towards Jerusalem. He got down on his knees three times a day and prayed and gave thanks before his God, as he had done previously. ... Then the king commanded, and Daniel was brought and

> cast into the den of lions. The king declared to Daniel, "May
> your God, whom you serve continually, deliver you!" …
> Then Daniel said to the king, "O king, live for ever! My God
> sent his angel and shut the lions' mouths, and they have not
> harmed me, because I was found blameless before him; and
> also before you, O king, I have done no harm." Then the
> king was exceedingly glad, and commanded that Daniel be
> taken up out of the den. So Daniel was taken up out of the
> den, and no kind of harm was found on him, because he
> had trusted in his God. (Daniel 6:3, 7, 10, 16, 21–23)

Nebuchadnezzar had taken God's people into captivity, but God showed him who was in control.

The prophecy of Ezekiel in the valley of dry bones is interesting in that we are told quite specifically that the Spirit of the Lord was leading the prophet, and the sovereignty of God is shown in a dramatic way in response to Ezekiel's prophecies. However, it is also important to note that the Spirit told Ezekiel what to prophesy and God then responded to his obedience.

> The hand of the Lord was upon me, and he brought me out
> in the Spirit of the Lord and set me down in the middle of
> the valley; it was full of bones. … So I prophesied as I was
> commanded. And as I prophesied, there was a sound, and
> behold, a rattling, and the bones came together, bone to
> its bone. And I looked, and behold, there were sinews on
> them, and flesh had come upon them, and skin had covered
> them. But there was no breath in them. Then he said to me,
> "Prophesy to the breath; prophesy, son of man, and say to
> the breath, Thus says the Lord God: Come from the four
> winds, O breath, and breathe on these slain, that they may
> live." So I prophesied as he commanded me, and the breath
> came into them, and they lived and stood on their feet, an
> exceedingly great army. … "And I will put my Spirit within
> you, and you shall live, and I will place you in your own

land. Then you shall know that I am the Lord; I have spoken, and I will do it, declares the Lord." (Ezekiel 37:1, 7–10, 14)

Moving into the New Testament gives us examples which may be nearer our own experience.

Acts 2 starts with the apostles—and possibly other believers—meeting together. We are not told why they had gathered, but it would seem reasonable to assume they had met as God's people—similar to an early form of "church service". It was almost certainly a spiritual occasion, rather than a purely social one. So it was in such an atmosphere that God entered and showed His sovereignty in two distinct ways.

Firstly, God chose this event to give His believers the Holy Spirit. The noise and the appearance of what looked like flames must have been awe-inspiring for those present. God would have done this to assure them that He was acting there.

Secondly, the use of languages meant that others would have been made aware that this was no ordinary day.

> When the day of Pentecost arrived, they were all together in one place. And suddenly there came from heaven a sound like a mighty rushing wind, and it filled the entire house where they were sitting. And divided tongues as of fire appeared to them and rested on each one of them. And they were all filled with the Holy Spirit and began to speak in other tongues as the Spirit gave them utterance. Now there were dwelling in Jerusalem Jews, devout men from every nation under heaven. And at this sound the multitude came together, and they were bewildered, because each one was hearing them speak in his own language. (Acts 2:1–6)

God's purpose in choosing to send His Spirit at Pentecost must have been related to the fact that the feast had brought men from all over the known world. The fact that they all heard the apostles speaking in their own respective languages probably differs from the normal speaking in tongues in that the apostles would have been talking in the Galilean dialect of Hebrew (or Aramaic) and were being heard in many languages at once. God was temporarily reversing the effects of Babel (Genesis 11).

Moving on, we find that the writer of the letter to the Hebrews lists the names of a large number of men of faith from the Old Testament. He describes the faithfulness of a number of them in some detail. He also lists many of the sufferings which they were willing to face in order to remain loyal to God. He finishes chapter 11 by telling his readers that they had not seen the outworking of God's sovereign plan of salvation. We have seen it, since we know of the coming of God's Son, Jesus, to bring us the reward of faith.

If those who lived before Jesus came could remain faithful to God, then we have more reason to do so. As we are told in Hebrews 11:39–40, "And all these, though commended through their faith, did not receive what was promised, since God had provided something better for us, that apart from us they should not be made perfect."

We must not leave this topic without looking at an amazing example of how God used the spirituality of a man to give us the most wonderful demonstration of His sovereignty in action. There are a few words tucked into the introduction of a mind-blowing book which are easily missed, yet they are crucial to the reading of the rest of the book: "I was in the Spirit on the Lord's day" (Revelation 1:10).

We are not told explicitly that God had not forced spirituality on John. It seems reasonable to assume that it was John's habit, and his own choice, to spend time in a close relationship with God, especially on the Lord's Day. It is because of this spiritual state that we can accept the Revelation as being from God. It was while John was in this spiritual state that God showed us, though him, that His sovereignty is way beyond our understanding and that His purposes for us, when Christ returns, cannot be thwarted.

THE SOVEREIGNTY OF GOD IN PREDESTINATION

Suggested Background Reading: Romans 8 and Ephesians 1

One of the great sources of disagreement in the church is that Christians hold views, often very fiercely, which are usually described as Calvinistic or Arminian. The common ground in the writings of Calvin and Arminius is too easily overlooked, and one issue is trumpeted—predestination. The details will follow, but at the heart of the discussion is the Calvinistic view that God chooses whom He will save, while the Arminians hold that we have the free will to accept, or reject, God's open offer of salvation.

The first consideration when looking at predestination is to decide what the word actually means. It is often used interchangeably with *election*, but is this correct? As with all such questions, we need to consider how the words are used in scripture.

The word *predestined* in scripture is used only by Paul, and in two of his letters (twice each).

In Romans 8:28–30, Paul writes the following:

> And we know that for those who love God all things work together for good, for those who are called according to his purpose. For those whom he foreknew he also predestined to be conformed to the image of his Son, in order that he might be the firstborn among many brothers. And those whom he predestined he also called, and those whom he called he also justified, and those whom he justified he also glorified.

To the Ephesians, in 1:3–12, he writes:

> Blessed be the God and Father of our Lord Jesus Christ, who has blessed us in Christ with every spiritual blessing in the heavenly places, even as he chose us in him before the foundation of the world, that we should be holy and blameless before him. In love he predestined us for adoption as sons through Jesus Christ, according to the purpose of his will, to the praise of his glorious grace, with which he has blessed us in the Beloved. In him we have redemption through his blood, the forgiveness of our trespasses, according to the riches of his grace, which he lavished upon us, in all wisdom and insight making known to us the mystery of his will, according to his purpose, which he set forth in Christ as a plan for the fullness of time, to unite all things in him, things in heaven and things on earth.

> In him we have obtained an inheritance, having been predestined according to the purpose of him who works all things according to the counsel of his will, so that we who were the first to hope in Christ might be to the praise of his glory.

These passages, themselves, are the cause of some disagreement.

Let's consider the Romans verses first. One school of thought considers the context. The Holy Spirit comes before God on our behalf because

He knows what we should be praying for so that everything will work for the good of God's people. This is because God knows who will respond to His call. He has declared that His people would be conformed to the image of His Son, so He has called them, justified them, and glorified them.

The alternative view is that the *knew* part of *foreknew* means the same as the word *knew* in the context of (for example) Genesis 4:1: "Now Adam *knew* Eve his wife, and she conceived and bore Cain" (emphasis mine).

The argument here is that *foreknow* means that God poured out His love on those whom He had chosen and that the predestination, calling, justification, and glorification followed by His will alone.

This latter view is not supported by the *Complete Jewish Bible*. One might expect a Hebrew-speaking Jewish translator, in this case David H. Stern, to understand the nuances of the Hebrew text better than somebody who learnt Hebrew as a second language. He translates Genesis 4:1 as "The man had sexual relations with Havah his wife", while "those whom He foreknew" is rendered "those whom he knew in advance". This breaks the link between the two words *knew* (in the sense of intimacy) and *foreknew*. This translation is also supported by W. E. Vine (*Expository Dictionary of New Testament Words*).

If one reads the word *predestination* in Romans as saying that God has a predetermined plan for those who accept His offer of salvation— and He knows in advance who they are—then one can read the same into what Paul wrote to the Ephesians. God chose to bless those who (as He knew before the foundation of the world) would accept Him by adopting us as sons and daughters, giving us redemption, forgiveness, and an inheritance. Ephesians 1:5 tells us that "He predestined *us*." The *us* here could be those whom God has chosen or, equally (if we approach this with an open mind), those who have chosen to accept God's offer of salvation.

All this may cast a new light on the meaning of *predestination*, but we must be careful not to assume that this leads us to the conclusion that it ends the debate about free will. What it does do is to direct us to clarify our terminology. What we should be doing, surely, is talking about *election* rather than predestination. The first view of predestination suggests that predestination and election mean the same thing. The second view points to predestination as the planning of blessings to follow salvation—whether that comes by election or free will.

The word *predestination* can be unhelpful, therefore. It seems appropriate to set the word aside at this point and consider the relationship between *election* and free will. It would also seem sensible to define our terms a little further. This discussion will consider the relevant positions of Calvin and Arminius in overview, but the underlying question is about conversion. Do we have the free will to accept or reject the salvation offered to us by God, or has He exercised His sovereign will to elect us—or otherwise—before Creation? To this end, let us look at the two arguments separately, without taking sides, and then put them together and see where we end up. We will study the scriptural basis for each view. We should also look at some views called Amyraldianism, which is sometimes referred to as four-point Calvinism. The following are the theological views, offered without any prejudice.

Question 21. *If two opposing views are both based on scripture, can either be correct?*

Calvinism

Those who uphold the view that God's people are elected through His sovereign grace alone are usually referred to as Calvinists.

John Calvin (1509–1564) was a French Reformer who became a highly respected theologian of the Reformation and has been commemorated in a tribute to the Reformers in Geneva, where a wall depicts them in bas-relief. He systematically expounded the Christian faith and is often considered to be one of the great theologians in the history of the church.

Calvin's theology is sometimes referred to as "Reformed" or, more usually, simply as "Calvinistic" and is often thought of as the opposite of Arminianism. Calvinism generally states that election is enshrined in God's sovereignty.

Calvin's theology is often summarised in the acronym TULIP. This stands for:

Total depravity
Unconditional election
Limited atonement
Irresistible grace
Perseverance of the saints

Let us look at each of these.

Total Depravity

This is the sinful nature we have inherited from Adam. "For as in Adam all die" (1 Corinthians 15:22)

In our natures, we totally lack spiritual good before a holy God. "For I know that nothing good dwells in me, that is, in my flesh. For I have the desire to do what is right, but not the ability to carry it out" (Romans 7:18).

In our actions, we are totally unable to do spiritual good before God. "For I do not do the good I want, but the evil I do not want is what I keep on doing" (Romans 7:19).

Unconditional Election

Wayne Grudem (*Systematic Theology*) defines *election* as "an act of God before creation in which He chooses some people to be saved, not on account of any foreseen merit in them, but only because of His sovereign good pleasure". Grudem summarises this as "God's choice of people to be saved".

The basic facts about election, in practice, as seen by Calvin, are the following:

1. Election is not based on God's foreknowledge of our faith.
2. Election is based on no facts other than God's foreknowledge of persons.
3. Scripture never speaks of our faith as the reason God chose us.
4. Election based on something good in us (such as our faith) would be the beginning of salvation by merit and thus would not be scriptural.
5. Predestination based on foreknowledge still does not give people free choice.

These statements lead us to the conclusion that election is unconditional.

Election is seen as the first of ten stages in the life of the Christian. The first six stages are related, in order, to becoming a Christian:

1. Election (God's choice of people to be saved)   ·

   "Even as *he chose us* in him before the foundation of the world, that we should be holy and blameless before him" (Ephesians 1:4; emphasis mine).

2. The gospel call (proclaiming the message of the gospel)

   "You may proclaim the excellencies of him who *called you* out of darkness into his marvellous light" (1 Peter 2:9; emphasis mine).

3. Regeneration (being born again)

Jesus answered him, "Truly, truly, I say to you, unless one is born again he cannot see the kingdom of God." Nicodemus said to him, "How can a man be born when he is old? Can he enter a second time into his mother's womb and be born?" Jesus answered, "Truly, truly, I say to you, unless one is born of water and the Spirit, he cannot enter the kingdom of God. That which is born of the flesh is flesh, and that which is born of the Spirit is spirit. Do not marvel that I said to you, 'You must be born again.'" (John 3:3–7)

4. Conversion (faith and repentance)

"But to all who did receive him, who believed in his name, he gave the right to become children of God, who were *born*, not of blood nor of the will of the flesh nor of the will of man, but *of God*" (John 1:12–13; emphasis mine).

5. Justification (right legal standing)

"Who shall bring any charge against *God's elect? It is God who justifies.* Who is to condemn?" (Romans 8:33–34; emphasis mine).

6. Adoption (membership in God's family)

"For you did not receive the spirit of slavery to fall back into fear, but you have received the Spirit of *adoption* as sons, by whom we cry, 'Abba! Father!'" (Romans 8:15; emphasis mine).

The next two are the outworking of Christianity:

7. Sanctification (right conduct of life)

"But now that you have been set free from sin and have become slaves of God, the fruit you get leads to sanctification and its end, eternal life" (Romans 6:22).

8. Perseverance (remaining a Christian)

> "For I have come down from heaven, not to do my own will but the will of him who sent me. And this is the will of him who sent me, that I should lose nothing of all that he has given me, but raise it up on the last day. For this is the will of my Father, that everyone who looks on the Son and believes in him should have eternal life, and I will raise him up on the last day" (John 6:38–40) (Perseverance is considered in more detail below, under the heading "Perseverance of the Saints".)

The ninth is at the end of this life:

9. Death (going to be with the Lord)

> "For to me to live is Christ, and to die is gain" (Philippians 1:21).

And finally, when Christ returns, comes this:

10. Glorification (receiving a resurrection body)

> "So is it with the resurrection of the dead. What is sown is perishable; what is raised is imperishable. It is sown in dishonour; it is raised in glory. It is sown in weakness; it is raised in power. It is sown a natural body; it is raised a spiritual body. If there is a natural body, there is also a spiritual body" (1 Corinthians 15:42–44).

The practical application of the doctrine of election is that I am a Christian because God has decided to set His love upon me. This should not be thought of as fatalistic or mechanistic (though Arminians would claim otherwise).

The Doctrine of Reprobation

The doctrine of reprobation is used to fill in the gaps left by election. It is the sovereign decision of God before Creation to pass over some persons, in sorrow deciding not to save them and to punish them for their sins and, thereby, to manifest His justice.

Limited Atonement

Some theologians prefer the term *particular redemption,* which means that redemption is given to the elect. These theologians consider that the term *limited atonement* is ambiguous. It is intended to state that atonement is limited to the elect but can be taken as suggesting that atonement may be incomplete.

There are many scripture passages which are used to support the Reformed view that atonement is for the elect only, and for them it is complete. Some examples are as follows:

> All that the Father gives me will come to me, and whoever comes to me I will never cast out. For I have come down from heaven, not to do my own will but the will of him who sent me. And this is the will of him who sent me, that I should lose nothing of all that he has given me, but raise it up on the last day. (John 6:37–39)

> I am the good shepherd. The good shepherd lays down his life for the sheep. ... Just as the Father knows me and I know the Father; and I lay down my life for the sheep. (John 10:11, 15)

> I am praying for them. I am not praying for the world but for those whom you have given me, for they are yours. (John 17:9)

> But God shows his love for us in that while we were still sinners, Christ died for us. Since, therefore, we have now been justified by his blood, much more shall we be saved by

him from the wrath of God. For if while we were enemies we were reconciled to God by the death of his Son, much more, now that we are reconciled, shall we be saved by his life. (Romans 5:8–10)

He who did not spare his own Son but gave him up for us all, how will he not also with him graciously give us all things? Who shall bring any charge against God's elect? It is God who justifies. Who is to condemn? Christ Jesus is the one who died—more than that, who was raised—who is at the right hand of God, who indeed is interceding for us. (Romans 8:32–34)

The Lord Jesus Christ, who gave himself for our sins to deliver us from the present evil age, according to the will of our God and Father. (Galatians 1:4)

Even as he chose us in him before the foundation of the world, that we should be holy and blameless before him. In love he predestined us for adoption as sons through Jesus Christ, according to the purpose of his will, to the praise of his glorious grace, with which he has blessed us in the Beloved. In him we have redemption through his blood, the forgiveness of our trespasses, according to the riches of his grace. (Ephesians 1:4–7)

For by grace you have been saved through faith. And this is not your own doing; it is the gift of God. (Ephesians 2:8)

There are a couple of points which need to be treated with care. (See also the comments on Amyraldianism, below.)

Firstly, there is a sense in which the statements "Christ died for His people only" and "Christ died for all people" are both true, though this concept might be more easily understood by an Arminian than a Calvinist. Here are some of the relevant scriptures:

I am the living bread that came down from heaven. If
anyone eats of this bread, he will live for ever. And the
bread that I will give for the life of the world is my flesh.
(John 6:51)

Christ Jesus, who gave himself as a ransom for all, which
is the testimony given at the proper time. (1 Timothy 2:6)

He is the propitiation for our sins, and not for ours only but
also for the sins of the whole world. (1 John 2:2)

Secondly, there is the risk of concentrating so hard on the purpose
of the Father and Son that we lose sight of what actually happened
in the Atonement.

Irresistible Grace

Sometimes the term *irresistible grace* is used by Calvinists to refer to the
fact that God effectively calls people and also gives them regeneration.
Both actions guarantee that we will respond in saving faith. The
term is subject to misunderstanding, however, since it *seems* to imply
that people do not make a voluntary, willing choice in responding to
the gospel—a wrong idea, and a wrong understanding of the term
irresistible grace. The term does preserve something valuable, however,
because it indicates that God's work reaches into our hearts to bring
about a response that is absolutely certain, even though we respond
voluntarily.

An "absolutely certain" "voluntary" response seems to give weight to
the view that God predestined those whom He "knew in advance"
would respond to Him, rather than those whom He chose to receive
His love.

Perseverance of the Saints

This part of Calvinism states that all who are truly born again will
persevere to the end and that only those who persevere to the end
have been truly born again.

The corollary is that those who finally fall away may give many external signs of conversion which are not genuine.

This can lead to a feeling of insecurity in the Christian since it suggests that one's Christian experience may not be real. The response to that would be to seek assurance by looking for a present trust in Christ for salvation, evidence of a regenerating work of the Holy Spirit in the heart, and a long-term pattern of growth in the Christian life.

The problem with this line of reasoning is that it leads us to judge as false a confession of faith by one who has since fallen away. Since we are told by our Lord Himself not to judge others, it is hard to hold this view of backsliding.

As we read in Luke 6:37, "Judge not, and you will not be judged; condemn not, and you will not be condemned; forgive, and you will be forgiven."

Amyraldianism

Amyraldianism is system of theology introduced by Moise Amyraut (1596–1664, also known in Latin as Moyses Amyraldus, and in English texts often Moses Amyraut. He was a French Protestant theologian, a metaphysician, and a professor of theology at Saumur). Amyraut held that the Calvinist doctrines of total depravity, unconditional election, irresistible grace, and perseverance of the saints are affirmed, along with (contrary to Calvinism) the teaching that Christ died savingly for all people, making salvation hypothetically possible for all, while only the elect are brought to faith and actually saved.

Amyraldianism suggests that God wills the salvation of all humankind on condition of faith whilst, at the same time, He wills the salvation of the elect specifically and unconditionally. In order to resolve this difficulty, it is argued that faith is a condition of God's will for salvation and that God has not willed the salvation of someone who has no faith.

Amyraldianism is sometimes called Amyraldism, hypothetical redemption, hypothetical universalism, four-point Calvinism, or post-redemptionism.

Arminianism

James Arminius (1560–1609) was a Reformed pastor in Amsterdam who later became professor of theology at the University of Leyden. His writings were assembled after his death but are not organised as a systematic theology in the same way as those of Calvin. They do, however, contain discussions of many important theological topics. His disagreement with some of the central tenets of Calvinism led to a great controversy in the Netherlands, which continued long after his death and is still at the heart of many disagreements today. His ideas became the foundation of a system of thought now known as Arminianism, which is sometimes referred to as "nonreformed" and which continues today in conservative Wesleyan and Methodist churches and in many other Protestant groups.

The Arminian position asserts the freedom of humankind to accept or reject the salvation offered by God through faith in Jesus. The main tenets of Arminianism are as follows:

1. The verses cited by the Calvinists as examples of God's providential control are exceptions and do not describe the way that God ordinarily works in human activity.
2. The Calvinist view wrongly makes God responsible for sin.
3. Choices caused by God cannot be real choices.
4. The Arminian view encourages responsible Christian living, while the Calvinistic view encourages a dangerous fatalism.
5. Not all evangelical theologians agree that we are counted guilty because of Adam's sin. Some, especially Arminian theologians, think this to be unfair of God and do not believe that it is taught in Romans 5. However, evangelicals of all persuasions do agree that we receive a sinful disposition or a tendency to sin as an inheritance from Adam.

6. An Arminian understanding of common grace gives to every person the *ability* to turn to God in faith and repentance and, in fact, *influences* the sinner to do this unless he or she specifically resist it. Therefore, on an Arminian understanding, common grace has a function that much more clearly relates to saving grace. In fact, common grace is simply an early expression of the totality of saving grace. This position holds that the ability to repent and believe is given to all people.

7. Arminians object to the doctrine of election for the following reasons:
   a. Election means that we do not have a choice in whether we accept Christ or not.
   b. With this definition of election, our choices are not real choices.
   c. The doctrine of election makes us puppets or robots, not real persons.
   d. The doctrine of election means that unbelievers never had a chance to believe.
   e. Election is unfair.
   f. The Bible says that God wills to save everyone.

8. Many Arminians have held that it is possible for someone who is truly born again to lose his or her salvation, while Reformed Christians have held that it is not possible for someone who is *truly* born again. (See point P of TULIP, above.)

9. Arminian theologians frequently assume that if they affirm human responsibility and the need for continuing in faith, they have thereby negated the idea that God's sovereign keeping and protection is absolutely certain and eternal life is guaranteed. But they often do this without providing any other convincing interpretation for the texts cited to demonstrate the doctrine of perseverance of the saints, and without providing any explanation that would show why we should not take these words as absolute guarantees that those who are born again will certainly persevere to the end. Rather than assuming that the passages on human responsibility negate the idea of God's sovereign protection,

we would do better to adopt the Reformed position that says that God's sovereign protection is consistent with human responsibility because it works through human responsibility and guarantees that we will respond by maintaining the faith that is necessary to persevere.

10. Arminians have argued that the branches (of the Vine) that do not bear fruit are still true branches of the Vine. Jesus refers to "every branch *of mine* that bears no fruit" (John 15:2; emphasis mine).

11. Therefore, the branches that are gathered and thrown into the fire and burned must refer to true believers who were once part of the Vine but fell away and became subject to eternal damnation.

Some of the scripture passages used to support the nonreformed view ("unlimited atonement" or "general redemption") are as follows:

Isaiah 56, the whole chapter, especially verses 6–7.

And the foreigners who join themselves to the Lord, to minister to him, to love the name of the Lord, and to be his servants, *everyone* who keeps the Sabbath and does not profane it, and holds fast my covenant—these I will bring to my holy mountain, and make them joyful in my house of prayer; their burnt offerings and their sacrifices will be accepted on my altar; for my house shall be called a house of prayer for all peoples. (Isaiah 56:6–7; emphasis mine)

The next day he saw Jesus coming towards him, and said, "Behold, the Lamb of God, who takes away *the sin of the world*!" (John 1:29; emphasis mine).

For God so loved *the world*, that he gave his only Son, that *whoever* believes in him should not perish but have eternal life. (John 3:16; emphasis mine)

For if your brother is grieved by what you eat, you are no longer walking in love. By what you eat, do not destroy *the one for whom Christ died*. (Romans 14:15; emphasis mine)

And so by your knowledge this weak person is destroyed, *the brother for whom Christ died*. (1 Corinthians 8:11; emphasis mine)

Christ Jesus, who gave himself as *a ransom for all*, which is the testimony given at the proper time. (1 Timothy 2:6; emphasis mine)

But we see him who for a little while was made lower than the angels, namely Jesus, crowned with glory and honour because of the suffering of death, so that by the grace of God he might taste death *for everyone*. (Hebrews 2:9; emphasis mine)

How much worse punishment, do you think, will be deserved by the one who has spurned the Son of God, and has profaned the blood of the covenant by which he was sanctified, and has outraged the Spirit of grace? (Hebrews 10:29)

But false prophets also arose among the people, just as there will be false teachers among you, who will secretly bring in destructive heresies, even denying the Master who bought them, bringing upon themselves swift destruction. (2 Peter 2:1)

The Lord is not slow to fulfil his promise as some count slowness, but is patient towards you, *not wishing that any should perish*, but that all should reach repentance. (2 Peter 3:9; emphasis mine)

He is the propitiation for our sins, and not for ours only but also for the sins *of the whole world*. (1 John 2:2; emphasis mine)

Question 22. *Does science ever prove the scriptures to be wrong?*

Summary

The **Calvinist** holds that God is sovereign and that He elects those whom He will save. Key verses for the Calvinist might be:

> I am praying for them. I am not praying for the world but for those whom you have given me, for they are yours. (John 17:9)

> Even as he chose us in him before the foundation of the world, that we should be holy and blameless before him. (Ephesians 1:4)

The **Arminian** holds that the Calvinistic approach means that we need not evangelise if God has already made His choice of whom to elect, but He has sent us to the world. He wants everybody to accept His offer of salvation. Key verses for the Arminian might be:

> And he said to them, "Go into all the world and proclaim the gospel to the whole creation." (Mark 16:15)

> The Lord is not slow to fulfil his promise as some count slowness, but is patient towards you, not wishing that any should perish, but that all should reach repentance. (2 Peter 3:9)

If Both Calvinism and Arminianism Are Based on Scripture, Then Which Is Correct?

There are some points of agreement which should be noted:

1. Not everybody will be saved.
2. A free offer of the gospel can rightly be made to every person ever born.
3. All agree that Christ's death in itself, because He is the infinite Son of God, has infinite merit and is in itself sufficient to pay

the penalty of the sins of as many or as few as the Father and the Son decree.

4. In terms of pastoral care for those who have strayed away from their Christian profession, we should realise that Calvinists and Arminians (those who believe in the perseverance of the saints and those who think that Christians can lose their salvation) *will both counsel a "backslider" in the same way*. According to the Arminian, this person was a Christian at one time but is no longer a Christian. According to the Calvinist, he never really was a Christian in the first place and is not one now. But in both cases the biblical counsel given would be the same: "You do not appear to be a Christian now. You must repent of your sins and trust in Christ for your salvation!" Though the Calvinist and Arminian would differ on their interpretation of the previous history, they would both agree on what should be done in the present.

5. Both the Calvinist and Arminian would allow for the possibility that the "backslidden" person is truly born again and had just fallen into sin and doubt. But both would agree that it is pastorally wise to assume that the person is not a Christian until some evidence of present faith is forthcoming.

6. In terms of the practical pastoral effects of our words, both those who hold to particular redemption and those who hold to general redemption agree on several key points:
   • Both sincerely want to avoid implying that people will be saved whether they believe in Christ or not.
   • Both sides want to avoid implying that there might be some people who come to Christ for salvation but are turned away because Christ did not die for them.
   • Both sides want to avoid implying that God is hypocritical or insincere when He makes the free offer of the gospel.

Another View of "Which?"

We could also note that Jesus, Himself, appears to hold both views together. John 6:37 reads, "All that the Father gives me will come to me, and whoever comes to me I will never cast out." If we think of what Jesus is saying here, we could think of it like this: "All that the Father gives Me [election] will come to Me, and whoever comes to Me [free will], I will never cast out."

Jesus seems to be affirming *both* election and free will in the same breath. How can this be?

There are times when science helps us to understand our faith, rather than seeming to cause problems of its own. This may be one such time!

Many generations of teenagers at school have been taught about light energy. With the exception of anyone who is totally blind, we are all very sensitive to light and can understand, and experiment with, much of its behaviour. The teaching about its nature can be rather less straightforward. The following is the generally accepted— and generally taught—theory, though it is always possible to find a dissenter who thinks he or she knows best!

In Genesis 9:13, God states, "I have set my bow in the cloud, and it shall be a sign of the covenant between me and the earth." The dispersion of white light into its component colours, as in a rainbow, is a sure sign that light travels as waves. This fact is strengthened when a double rainbow is seen because there is no dispersed light between the two bows. Experiments which involve passing light through very narrow slits prove convincingly that light does, indeed, travel as a waveform. The fundamental evidence is that light can be seen to "cancel out" ("destructively interfere"), which could not possibly happen if light consisted of particles.

Many pieces of electrical equipment are powered by solar cells. A growing number of pocket calculators have them. Solar cells are also becoming increasingly popular on the roofs of houses and other buildings, and "solar farms" are springing up where solar energy is used as the fuel for electric power stations. The significance of these cells is that they prove that light travels as particles. Were light to travel as waves, these cells would not be able to generate electricity.

Since we have two contradictory views about the nature of light, our students are taught about the "wave–particle duality" of light. This effectively means that we use whichever description of light fits with what we are doing at the time, whilst respecting the fact that the alternative description also exists.

We could think of a train on a track with two rails. Removing either rail would lead to disaster!

The following story gives an insight into the way in which a father saved one lad and not another. He chose which lad to save. The one he saved had to respond to the lifeline offered. The story is *not* a good reflection on election in that God is not limited in how many people He can save.

The story is of an American pastor who interrupted his service one evening just before preaching his sermon to introduce a visiting minister. He said that the visitor had been a very good friend of his for many years, and he invited him to say a few words. At that, an elderly man rose slowly to his feet and shuffled forward to speak to the congregation. He told the following story:

"Many years ago there was a group of three—a man, his son, and a friend of the son—who went sailing from the West Coast of the United States and out onto the Pacific Ocean. All was well until a violent storm arose and their boat was hit by a large wave. The boat capsized, throwing all three of them into the sea. The father managed to hold onto the boat and grab a lifeline. He quickly realised that he could only save one of the lads and that he had to make a dreadful decision: Which of the lads should he save? The father knew that his son was a Christian and that the friend was not. He shouted 'I love you' to his son, over the noise of the storm, and then threw the lifeline to the friend and pulled him to the safety of the boat. As the father saw his son vanish beneath the waves, he knew that he would see him again in heaven as the lad would step into the presence of Jesus. Leaving the friend to pass into an eternity without Jesus was too awful to contemplate. He had sacrificed his own son in order to rescue the son's friend."

The visitor ended by reminding the congregation that God's love for us is so great that He had sacrificed His own Son so that we could be rescued. He encouraged those present to take hold of the lifeline that the Father was offering in that service. He then returned to his seat, and the pastor continued with his sermon.

Some teenagers who were in the church that evening had been looking disbelievingly as the elderly visitor spoke. Afterwards they approached him and told him that they did not feel the story to be very realistic. "No father would behave like that!"

"It may seem unlikely," came the old minister's reply. "But this story shows me something of the love of the Father for us. What I can tell you is that the father in the story is standing in front of you right now, and my son's friend is your pastor here."

In Conclusion

When we are faced with the challenge of accepting or rejecting God's offer of salvation through the shed blood of Jesus, no claim of "not having been elected" will be a valid excuse for our rejecting it. As we are asked in Hebrews 2:3, "How shall we escape if we neglect such a great salvation?"

Chapter 11

THE SOVEREIGNTY OF GOD IN RELATIONSHIPS

Suggested Background Reading: Ruth 1-4

It has been said that coincidence is God's way of staying anonymous. It is great to see and experience times when God is at work, providing all that we need—and more, quite often—and bringing His plans to fruition. Sometimes things happen which are quite unexpected and we wonder why, until we later see that God was working out a plan. A story will illustrate this:

I heard of a woman who was delayed by a road accident as she went to catch a train. She dashed into the train station to see the back of her train disappearing down the line. Her cry was "Praise the Lord!" She left the station.

She was back in the station in good time for the next train. A woman at the station spoke to her. "Most people would swear if they missed a train, but you said, 'Praise the Lord.' Why?" She missed the next train telling her!

Unfortunately, history does not relate the outcome of this conversation.

At other times God uses the ordinary things we do for His purposes. We never know when we are being watched.

In chapter 8, I told of a friend and I working in a hospital in London and involved in the Christian union there. As we started to eat, we were aware of a nurse standing beside us. We had not seen her before. She said, "You're Christians, aren't you? I thought so by the way you took your forks, so I watched to see if you stopped to give thanks before eating, which confirmed it. Is there a Christian union in this hospital?" It emerged that she was a Christian, but she had considerable needs—not least of all for strong Christian love and support.

In both these cases, God used events to bring people together for His purposes. In the first case, it was to reach out to somebody with the gospel. In the second case, it was to provide help, support, friendship, and protection for one of His own who was needy and vulnerable. This is God's providential sovereignty in action in relationships between people. In both cases, God had His people in the right place at the right time and doing the right thing, albeit unwittingly.

The story of Ruth is particularly interesting in the context of the sovereignty of God because God is mentioned so infrequently. Ruth refers to Him (twice) in chapter 1 verse 16 when declaring her allegiance to Him, and in the next chapter (verse 12) we read of Boaz responding to Ruth's loyalty to Naomi with the prayer that "the Lord, the God of Israel" would reward her. The book also contains a number of greetings such as "the Lord be with you" or "the Lord bless you" (2:4) and similar references to the Lord. We do not, however, read of God taking part in any active way in this book, except to give Ruth conception of a son (in 4:13). Nevertheless, it is quite clear that God is at work throughout the book, bringing His divine will to fruition. The whole story rings with His sovereignty. We could say the same about the book of Esther, where God is clearly in control the whole time but is never mentioned once.

If we look through the account of Ruth, we are immediately introduced to God's response to the sin of His people. This we learn from Judges 4, which starts with the words "And the people of Israel again did what was evil in the sight of the Lord after Ehud died." The book of Ruth is set shortly after this time. God's people were living in "a land flowing with milk and honey" (see Joshua 5:6—and nearly twenty other references) and were experiencing famine because God was reminding them that the bounty of the land came from Him. He was using His sovereignty over nature to draw His people back to Himself. God cherished His relationship with His people and disciplined them—in love and sorrow, rather than in anger.

The only reason that God could not wipe the Hebrew nation off the face of the earth was that He had made a covenant with them to raise up a Saviour from among them. In Ruth's day this was a promise awaiting fulfilment. God had chosen to fulfil that promise through David, the great-grandson of Ruth. At the time of the famine, Ruth was living in Moab and was unaware of who God was—or even of His existence. She probably knew no more than rumours about the Hebrew people as a nation.

It is later in the first chapter, after a family of God's people had gone to live in Moab and intermarried with the Moabites, and the women had all been widowed, where we read that Naomi "heard in the fields of Moab that the Lord had visited his people and given them food" (v. 6). So it is that we read of Naomi returning with Ruth to Judea. Not only that, but also their home city was none other than Bethlehem, the very city where Jesus was to be born because of the link with David. This had been prophesied long before, in Micah 5:2: "But you, Bethlehem Ephrathah, though you are little among the thousands of Judah, yet out of you shall come forth to Me the One to be Ruler in Israel, whose goings forth are from of old, from everlasting."

God is also at work—again behind the scenes—establishing a relationship between Ruth and Boaz. They first meet when Boaz sees Ruth gleaning in his field and he shows kindness to her, but by the end of chapter 2 it seems as if the relationship is over. However, God is still at work. In chapter 3, the possibility is raised that the relationship may progress, but there is a problem: another man who might marry Ruth, not the man Boaz whom God has planned for.

The last chapter of Ruth is a little less straightforward to understand until we remind ourselves of the offices of levirate and goel. (These were referred to earlier, in chapter 8). In both these offices we see God has given His people some rules for living which are designed to improve their lifestyle.

The office of levirate was given by God while His people were still in the wilderness:

> If brothers dwell together, and one of them dies and has no son, the wife of the dead man shall not be married outside the family to a stranger. Her husband's brother shall go in to her and take her as his wife and perform the duty of a husband's brother to her. And the first son whom she bears shall succeed to the name of his dead brother, that his name may not be blotted out of Israel. And if the man does not wish to take his brother's wife, then his brother's wife shall go up to the gate to the elders and say, "My husband's brother refuses to perpetuate his brother's name in Israel; he will not perform the duty of a husband's brother to me." Then the elders of his city shall call him and speak to him, and if he persists, saying, "I do not wish to take her," then his brother's wife shall go up to him in the presence of the elders and pull his sandal off his foot and spit in his face. And she shall answer and say, "So shall it be done to the man who does not build up his brother's house." And the name of his house shall be called in Israel, "The house of him who had his sandal pulled off." (Deuteronomy 25:5–10)

This was still being practised in the time of Jesus, as we see here:

> The same day Sadducees came to him, who say that there is no resurrection, and they asked him a question, saying, "Teacher, Moses said, 'If a man dies having no children, his brother must marry the widow and raise up children for his brother.' Now there were seven brothers among us. The first married and died, and having no children left his wife to his brother. So too the second and third, down to the seventh. After them all, the woman died. In the resurrection, therefore, of the seven, whose wife will she be? For they all had her." But Jesus answered them, "You are wrong, because you know neither the Scriptures nor the power of God. For in the resurrection they neither marry nor are given in marriage, but are like angels in heaven. And as for the resurrection of the dead, have you not read what was said to you by God: 'I am the God of Abraham, and the God of Isaac, and the God of Jacob'? He is not God of the dead, but of the living." And when the crowd heard it, they were astonished at his teaching. (Matthew 22:23–33)

Question 23. *Should we model our relationships with others on the relationships which Jesus had with others (e.g. money changers)?*

The office of goel, or kinsman redeemer, was also given to God's people before they had any land of their own.

> The land shall not be sold in perpetuity, for the land is mine. For you are strangers and sojourners with me. And in all the country you possess, you shall allow a redemption of the land. If your brother becomes poor and sells part of his property, then his nearest redeemer shall come and redeem what his brother has sold. If a man has no one to redeem it and then himself becomes prosperous and finds sufficient means to redeem it, let him calculate the years since he sold it and pay back the balance to the man

to whom he sold it, and then return to his property. But if he has not sufficient means to recover it, then what he sold shall remain in the hand of the buyer until the year of jubilee. In the jubilee it shall be released, and he shall return to his property. ...If a stranger or sojourner with you becomes rich, and your brother beside him becomes poor and sells himself to the stranger or sojourner with you or to a member of the stranger's clan, then after he is sold he may be redeemed. One of his brothers may redeem him, or his uncle or his cousin may redeem him, or a close relative from his clan may redeem him. Or if he grows rich he may redeem himself. (Leviticus 25:23–28, 47-49)

Clearly, it would be wrong to say that these laws were put in place only so that Ruth's relationship would be established with Boaz rather than the "nearer kinsman", but we can certainly say that God was using these laws for His purposes in this case. We can also be sure that God had given them a love for each other. We are told quite plainly that, when they married, the Lord gave Ruth conception and she bore a son.

God was working out His sovereign purposes by controlling the emotions of those involved and by manipulating the circumstances so they made decisions, apparently of their own free will, which led to His will being carried out.

The challenge for us is to be aware that God could be depending on us for anything by what we do or say or by our attitudes. The Bible is full of accounts of God bringing the right people together at the right time for both their good and His. Do we live our lives so that He can use us to relate to other people, and are we grateful when He uses our relationships with others to help us in our walk with Him?

Let us list some of the events in the book of Ruth which demonstrate God's sovereignty over everyday life by which He brought about Ruth and Boaz to be the great-grandparents of King David in Bethlehem:

- In Ruth 1:1, God sent famine by withholding His bounty to a "land flowing with milk and honey".
  The Hebrew nation was in a constant cycle of idolatry, oppression or other punishment (brought about by God), repentance, and restitution as God raised a "judge" to lead the people against the oppressor, followed by a period of peace, leading to complacency as the people forgot that it was God who had rescued them then went back to idolatry etc. In this case God has brought the famine at a time when the people were at peace with Moab.

- In Ruth 1:1, Elimelech and family go to Moab, where Ruth is. We are not told specifically why God determined to bring Ruth into His family. We do know that she was significant enough to warrant a mention by name in Matthew's genealogy of Jesus (Matthew 1:5). She is also a reminder that the Gospel is for Gentiles as well as Jews.

- In Ruth 1:2, we learn that the family of Elimelech were Ephrathites from Bethlehem in Judah, where Jesus was to be born. Micah (referred to above) was very specific that Christ would come from Bethlehem Ephrathah. The writer of the book of Ruth is equally specific. God was leaving nothing to chance. No other "Bethlehem" would do.

- In Ruth 1:4, Mahlon married Ruth.
  It is of no consequence which brother married Ruth. In fact we are not told which brother it was until the end of the book. The fact is that Ruth was brought into the family despite her Moabite citizenship. The Hebrews were forbidden to marry outside their own nation, so God was using Mahlon's sin for His own sovereign purposes.

- In Ruth 1:5, we read that Mahlon died childless.
  Had Ruth had a son by Mahlon (or anyone else other than Boaz), then the story would have been very different—the levirate marriage would not have been relevant.

- In Ruth 1:6, God provided food in Judea.
  The people reached the point in their cycle when God would restore them. This came at just the right time for Ruth to move from Moab to Bethlehem with Naomi.

- In Ruth 1:6, we read that Naomi had heard about God's provision of food.
  It would be quite remarkable for the rumour mill to reach faraway Moab.

- In Ruth 1:6, Naomi set out for Bethlehem.
  For two widows—the most vulnerable members of society— to make this journey unescorted and to arrive safely shows the providence of God in action.

- In Ruth 1:16–17, we read that Ruth remained loyal to Naomi.
  Ruth's expression of loyalty to Naomi, and also loyalty to God, indicates that Naomi or Mahlon must have taught her about God. This was still an extraordinary act of faith in God's providence.

- In Ruth 1:22, we read that they arrived at the optimum time.
  Arriving at the beginning of the barley harvest meant that they had the whole of the harvest period to gather food. The barley harvest would be followed by wheat harvest. They arrived in time for both.

- In Ruth 2:1, we learn that Boaz was already living in Bethlehem.
  God had a wealthy farmer ready to help the destitute widows.

- In Ruth 2:2, we discover that Ruth had learnt Jewish customs.
  Ruth had been taught about gleaning and could therefore take advantage of God's provision.

- In Ruth 2:3, Ruth "happened" to come to the part of the field belonging to Boaz.

We have been told about Boaz, but it seems from the text that Ruth was unaware of the existence of Boaz and of the fact that she was gleaning in his field.

- In Ruth 2:5, Boaz notices Ruth.
  There could have been a number of women in the field. They normally would have been ignored.

- In Ruth 2:8–9, we read that Boaz showed Ruth kindness and gave her protection.
  As a young widow, Ruth would have been quite vulnerable. The reapers would have represented a threat to her, but Boaz turned things round so that they became her protectors.

- In Ruth 2:11, we learn that Ruth's reputation had spread. The rumour mill had been busy.

- In Ruth 2:19–20, the family link is recognised. Naomi realised that Boaz was a kinsman.

- In Ruth 3:3–6, we see that the relationship became personal. The relationship is no longer just about gleaning. Ruth, at Naomi's direction, goes to see Boaz privately.

- In Ruth 3:9, we read that Ruth asked for redemption. Ruth is, effectively, asking for (levirate) marriage.

- In Ruth 3:9–10, though it has not be stated explicitly, it is clear that Ruth and Boaz have fallen in love.
  God is love!

- In Ruth 3:10, we read that Ruth remained loyal to the family. There must have been many pressures on Ruth to seek a relationship with a younger man, perhaps one of the reapers. Her relationship with God was a stronger pressure.

- In Ruth 3:13, Boaz expressed willingness to act as redeemer but told Ruth of a problem.
  God still had a problem to overcome.

- In Ruth 4:1, we read that Boaz went to the correct place to sort out legal matters.
  The gate was effectively the courtroom and a place for all sorts of business to be carried out.

- In Ruth 4:1, we read that the other kinsman passed that way. We are not told if he often went that way or if God directed his steps there on that day.

- In Ruth 4:2, Boaz took witnesses to keep the proceedings legal. God ensured that there would be no misunderstandings later. Boaz had plenty of witnesses.

- In Ruth 4:2, the other kinsman agreed to talk.
  He could easily have said that he was too busy or did not want to talk.

- In Ruth 4:6, we read that the other kinsman backed out. The other kinsman was prepared to bring shame on himself because he wanted to protect his name. Any son he had with Ruth would have been Mahlon's heir and not his. It could be noted that the man who wanted to protect his name is the only person of any significance in the story whose name we are not told.

- In Ruth 4:13, Ruth and Boaz were married. Once again, everything was done properly.

- In Ruth 4:13, we read that the Lord gave Ruth conception. Ruth had not had a child by Mahlon, so conceiving by Boaz was significant.

- In Ruth 4:13, we learn that the child was a son. Obed was the grandfather of David.

This list is not intended to be exhaustive, but these thirty statements describe events which are pointing us to God's sovereign hand at work. Had any one of these events not happened, then the whole plan of God could have been thwarted. Each event did take place because God was working in the background, bringing His plans into action. In many of these cases the event depended on the relationships between those involved.

God's plans will not be thwarted by our errors, but we may lose some of the blessings He seeks to shower upon us daily. Elimelech was in error by leaving Judea. Mahlon was in error when he married Ruth. God used both to bring Ruth to Boaz in Bethlehem.

We could also look at another example of God using the sin of human beings for His purposes. The book of Genesis tells us how Joseph was sold into slavery in Egypt by his brothers. We then read of Joseph saving the Egyptians from famine and of the whole of Joseph's family moving to Egypt. When their father died, Joseph's brothers were anxious that Joseph would take revenge on them for their treatment of him. They sent a message to Joseph claiming that their father had left a message for Joseph not to take revenge on them. (This was actually a lie.) However, Joseph had realised that God had allowed the events which took him to Egypt as part of His plan. We read this in Joseph's reply to the brothers: "But Joseph said to them, 'Do not fear, for am I in the place of God? As for you, you meant evil against me, but God meant it for good, to bring it about that many people should be kept alive, as they are today'" (Genesis 50:19–20).

Some of those who were kept alive were, of course, the brothers whom Joseph was talking to and their families. We are not told at which point in time Joseph realised that he was in Egypt as part of God's plan, but we are left in no doubt that "God meant it for good."

Another important example of God directing people behind the scenes to serve His own ends is found in the story of Esther. Nowhere in the canonical book is God mentioned by name. (The longer apocryphal version of the book, originally in Greek, does mention the name of God, but this version should not be treated as inspired by God as is the canonical version.)

The essence of the story is that the Jews were in exile in Persia and that Esther had become queen. A plot to exterminate the Jews was hatched by an official (Haman) who hated those who did not bow down to him.

A Jew (Mordecai) who had heard of the plot sent a message to Esther telling her to seek help by going to the king—even though going to him uninvited meant risking her life. Mordecai urged her to take that risk with words which expressed the sovereignty of God to save the people through whom he had covenanted to provide a Redeemer. Esther 4:14 reads, "For if you keep silent at this time, relief and deliverance will rise for the Jews from another place, but you and your father's house will perish. And who knows whether you have not come to the kingdom for such a time as this?"

God was clearly acting behind the scenes as Esther was accepted into the king's presence and the people were saved.

The relationships between the various people involved here are very important.

Mordecai was well respected in the community and was in a place to hear about the plot against the Jews. This gave him the ability to send messages to Esther in the palace.

Also, Mordecai was the cousin of Esther, but he had adopted her as his daughter so Esther would be prepared to take his warnings seriously.

The relationships between Esther and God and between Mordecai and God were vital to God's plan to save His people. Both were in the right place at the right time for God to use, and both were prepared to act as God directed.

The plan also depended on the relationship between Esther and the king. Had the king not had a great love for Esther, she would almost certainly have lost her life.

It could be argued that the relationship between the king and his former queen, Vashti, was in God's hands too. She refused to obey the king's command to appear at his feast, so she was deposed. This opened the way for Esther to become queen and be in place "for such a time as this".

Another part of God's plan to save His people is seen when the conspirators cast lots to choose a date when the Jews would be attacked. The lot was for a day sufficiently far in the future for a rescue plan to be achieved. God showed that He was at work even in the rolling of dice!

Relationships are essential to God's plan even when they are, so to speak, in the background. God's covenant relationship with Abraham made it clear that the Messiah would be a descendant of his: "In your offspring shall all the nations of the earth be blessed, because you have obeyed my voice" (Genesis 22:18).

It was important to God that Jesus be a blood relative of the man to whom He had given His covenant. As we read in Genesis 15:4, "Behold, the word of the Lord came to him: 'This man [Eliezer of Damascus] shall not be your heir; *your very own son* shall be your heir'" (emphasis mine).

When we turn to the prophecies concerning the coming of Jesus, we see that the relationship which God ordained to exist between Jesus and Jesse (father of David) was twofold. As we read in Isaiah 11:1,

"There shall come forth a shoot from the stump of Jesse, and a branch from his roots shall bear fruit."

God has ensured that His covenant will be kept—and be seen to be kept. Jesse is the grandson of Ruth and Boaz, and the father of David.

The only blood relative that Jesus had was Mary. Mary was the daughter of Heli, a direct descendant of Nathan, son of David, son of Jesse, so Jesus was a blood relative of Jesse and, therefore, of Abraham. This genealogy is to be found in Luke 3.

The Jewish authorities of the day would have recorded Joseph as the father of Jesus, however, since mothers were not normally recorded in ancestral records. God had this in mind, too, and He chose Joseph as the recorded father. Joseph was a direct descendant of Solomon, also a son of David. This genealogy is recorded for us at the start of Matthew's Gospel. Thus, Jesus was descended "root and branch" from Jesse, just as Isaiah had prophesied.

It is also worth noting that Jesus came when He did. About forty years after He returned to His Father, the Romans destroyed the Temple in Jerusalem, which is where the records of births would have been kept.

Another example of God exercising His sovereign will in family relationships is seen in the brothers Esau and Jacob. These brothers were twins—and rivals. We read that the rivalry started even before they were born. This was evident again as they were born with Jacob holding the heel of his firstborn brother.

> Isaac prayed to the Lord for his wife, because she was barren. And the Lord granted his prayer, and Rebekah his wife conceived. The children struggled together within her, and she said, "If it is thus, why is this happening to me?" So she went to enquire of the Lord. And the Lord said to her, "Two nations are in your womb, and two peoples from within you shall be divided; the one shall be stronger than

167

the other, the older shall serve the younger." When her days to give birth were completed, behold, there were twins in her womb. The first came out red, all his body like a hairy cloak, so they called his name Esau. Afterwards his brother came out with his hand holding Esau's heel, so his name was called Jacob. (Genesis 25:21–26)

The fact that Esau was born first meant that he should have been Isaac's heir. This was not the way God wanted it—He wanted Jacob to be the heir—so we read of more unexpected events which brought God's will to pass.

Firstly, Jacob cheated his brother and bought the birthright for a bowl of stew (Genesis 25). This was pretty disgraceful behaviour on the part on both of them, but it did give Jacob the inheritance.

Secondly, Jacob cheated Esau out of their father's dying blessing (Genesis 27), which was effectively when Isaac handed over the inheritance to what he thought was his elder son.

An example of a very different sort of relationship is of that between David and Goliath:

And when the Philistine looked and saw David, he disdained him, for he was but a youth, ruddy and handsome in appearance. ... When the Philistine arose and came and drew near to meet David, David ran quickly towards the battle line to meet the Philistine. And David put his hand in his bag and took out a stone and slung it and struck the Philistine on his forehead. The stone sank into his forehead, and he fell on his face to the ground. (1 Samuel 17:42, 48–49)

This is an example of a relationship between enemies, but what is remarkable is that the relationship is very unbalanced. On the face of it we have a giant, who was a seasoned warrior and who was very well armed and protected, pitted against a young lad who had no more than a sling and a few stones. On closer inspection, however, we do, indeed, behold a very unbalanced relationship, but the balance is on the other side, because although David seems to have virtually nothing to fight with, he is acting within God's sovereign will, which is more than enough to defeat the giant. We need to note that God did not strike the giant down. What He did was to guide David, and the stone, to achieve His will.

This should be a lesson for us. God uses us to bring His plans to fruition, and we may need to step out in faith for this to occur, even though the task may seem beyond us.

The letter which Paul wrote to Philemon about his slave Onesimus gives us an insight into a series of relationships. Onesimus had run away from his master, Philemon, so that relationship had been broken. Philemon would have been legally entitled to have Onesimus put to death.

Onesimus had met up with Paul and become his brother in Christ. Paul would have liked to keep Onesimus with him, but he realised that he had to return to Philemon.

Paul, who knew Philemon as a fellow Christian, appealed to him as such on behalf of Onesimus.

All three had a relationship with God as His children, newly so in the case of Onesimus.

> Accordingly, though I am bold enough in Christ to command you to do what is required, yet for love's sake I prefer to appeal to you—I, Paul, an old man and now a prisoner also for Christ Jesus—I appeal to you for my child, Onesimus, whose father I became in my imprisonment. (Formerly he was useless to you, but now he is indeed useful to you and to me.) I am sending him back to you, sending my very heart. I would have been glad to keep him with me, in order that he might serve me on your behalf during my

imprisonment for the gospel, but I preferred to do nothing without your consent in order that your goodness might not be by compulsion but of your own accord. For this perhaps is why he was parted from you for a while, that you might have him back for ever, no longer as a slave but more than a slave, as a beloved brother—especially to me, but how much more to you, both in the flesh and in the Lord. So if you consider me your partner, receive him as you would receive me. If he has wronged you at all, or owes you anything, charge that to my account. I, Paul, write this with my own hand: I will repay it—to say nothing of your owing me even your own self. Yes, brother, I want some benefit from you in the Lord. Refresh my heart in Christ. Confident of your obedience, I write to you, knowing that you will do even more than I say. At the same time, prepare a guest room for me, for I am hoping that through your prayers I will be graciously given to you. (Philemon 8–22)

Question 24. *If God is sovereign over our emotions, why are we not always happy?*

Relationships do not always have to be between people. God sometimes uses plants or animals to carry out His commands.

We saw in chapter 5 that God sent Elijah to King Ahab to tell him of coming famine. God had a plan to protect Elijah during that time:

> "You shall drink from the brook, and I have commanded the ravens to feed you there." So he went and did according to the word of the Lord. He went and lived by the brook Cherith that is east of the Jordan. And the ravens brought him bread and meat in the morning, and bread and meat in the evening, and he drank from the brook. (1 Kings 17:4–6)

The relationship between Elijah and the ravens was a matter of life and death for the prophet.

There has been at least one case in recent times of birds being the lifeline for human beings.

In 1942, the crew of a B-17 Flying Fortress had to ditch their aircraft in the South Pacific. Long after their emergency ration had run out, and when the men were on the point of starvation, one of them, Captain Eddie Rickenbacker, pulled his cap over his face and began to doze off. He felt something land on his head, which turned out to be a seagull. He managed to catch the bird, which was eaten by the men, the intestines being used for bait for fishing.

All the men were eventually rescued.

So the question comes to us: Are we aware of what God is doing in our lives, especially in the way we interact with other people, for our benefit or the benefit of others, or for God's benefit?

We have many types of relationships, such as the following:

- husband–wife
- boy–girl
- parent–child
- sibling to sibling
- employer–employee
- colleague to colleague
- teacher–pupil
- neighbour to neighbour
- bus driver–passenger
- pastor–church member–church visitor
- with the taxman
- with a passing stranger in the street
- us–nature
- author–reader
- self–God

It may be that any such relationship has been put there by God because He has a special purpose for it. We need to be sensitive to His direction and let Him guide us in any relationship we may have with other people, whoever they may be.

We should never lose sight of the fact that the most important relationship each of us has is with our sovereign Creator. If we are His children, then we must remember that we have that wonderful relationship with Him at a tremendous cost—He paid for it with the blood of His Son. This is the relationship which He seeks most of all. At the time of the Fall, Adam and Eve "heard the sound of the Lord God walking in the garden in the cool of the day" (Genesis 3:8). Prior to that, God would walk with Adam and Eve. There would have been a very close companionship amongst them, a very precious relationship indeed. This relationship is the purpose of Creation.

We have already considered why God allowed sin to spoil His relationship with His people, but the whole of scripture tells of how God is restoring that relationship to its former state. Meanwhile we can know what it is to have a relationship with Him, though it is rather less than He originally intended and rather less than it will be when we meet Him face to face.

Our response should be actively to seek to strengthen our relationship with God and to strive to bring others into such a relationship for the salvation of their souls—and for the glory of God.

THE SOVEREIGNTY OF GOD IN ACTIONS

Suggested Background Reading: Acts 5

W hen we consider the sovereignty of God in actions, we need to be careful to understand whose actions we are talking about.

If we consider God's actions, we may simply say that God, in His sovereignty, is able to act in any way He pleases. Since He can never undertake any action which may contain any sort of evil, we must see that it is His pleasure to do good, but His pleasure may be in the immediate effect of the action, such as giving a blessing to one of His children, or in the long-term effect of that action, such as sending His Son to the cross.

For us it is more significant to ask ourselves how our actions are affected by God's sovereignty.

As we saw in the study on predestination, there are times when we must understand that God is sovereign and directs our every move, and then there are times when we make choices of our own free will, take responsibility for our actions, and face the consequences of them.

In Acts 5 we read of Ananias and Sapphira. Ananias was a man who did a very good thing and then a very bad thing. He sold a piece of land and took some of the proceeds to the apostles. This was highly commendable. He was perfectly entitled to keep some of the money back for himself. He could have kept it all had he wanted to. Where he went wrong was in claiming that the money he had brought was the total raised by the sale. The wrong action was lying to God. God did not force him to lie, as that would mean that God brought about an evil act. God did punish Ananias for lying.

The same is true of Sapphira, when she appeared three hours later. Peter asked her directly if the money that Ananias had brought was the full income from the sale, and she said that it was. She chose to lie. God did not force her to lie, and He did punish her for doing so.

It does happen very occasionally that people die very suddenly, with no prior warning at all. One could argue, therefore, that the death of Ananias was just such a death. It would be a remarkable coincidence that he died in an unusual way at exactly that moment. It is inconceivable, however, that the same should happen to both Ananias and Sapphira in such a circumstance and being so close together. We are left with the only sensible explanation for these deaths: the sovereign God intervened and delivered punishment.

The word *punishment* in this context needs to be qualified. The purpose of God's actions in taking the lives of Ananias and Sapphira so abruptly must have been to send a clear message to all those around that He was the sovereign God, that He did know what was happening on earth, and that He should not be lied to.

And great fear came upon all who heard of it. (Acts 5:5)

And great fear came upon the whole church and upon all who heard of these things. (Acts 5:11)

Whilst this would have been seen as harsh punishment to the observers, we must remember that these were God's people who therefore would have immediately entered the presence of God in His glory. Seen in this way, the instant departure of Ananias and Sapphira, without a long and painful illness first, may begin to seem more like a reward than a punishment, but in no way does this excuse their actions.

The events involving Ananias and Sapphira, and the "many signs and wonders" done by the apostles, had a dramatic effect on the wider community in Jerusalem and the surrounding towns. Many people came to believe in the Lord as a result of seeing God's sovereignty at work.

Against this backdrop, the jealousy of the authorities would not come as a surprise, but their actions in putting the apostles in prison did not change God's plans. His angel brought the apostles out of the prison while the gates remained locked and the guards were in place. God's sovereignty was shown to be greater than the authority of the Sadducees.

When the apostles were arrested again for preaching about Jesus, God raised up somebody to stand up and talk some sense to the Sadducees. He was "a Pharisee in the council named Gamaliel, a teacher of the law held in honour by all the people" (Acts 5:34). His action in support of the apostles meant that they were able to continue preaching.

Situations where God's sovereignty was demonstrated by the actions of one person can be found in many parts of the Old Testament.

When God called Moses to lead His people out of Egypt, He gave him three powerful signs. These, in themselves, tell us of God's sovereignty over nature. We are also told that they were to convince the people that God had, indeed, called Moses to be their leader.

> The Lord said to him, "What is that in your hand?" He said, "A staff." And he said, "Throw it on the ground." So he threw it on the ground, and it became a serpent, and

Moses ran from it. But the Lord said to Moses, "Put out your hand and catch it by the tail"—so he put out his hand and caught it, and it became a staff in his hand—"that they may believe that the Lord, the God of their fathers, the God of Abraham, the God of Isaac, and the God of Jacob, has appeared to you." Again, the Lord said to him, "Put your hand inside your cloak." And he put his hand inside his cloak, and when he took it out, behold, his hand was leprous like snow. Then God said, "Put your hand back inside your cloak." So he put his hand back inside his cloak, and when he took it out, behold, it was restored like the rest of his flesh. "If they will not believe you," God said, "or listen to the first sign, they may believe the latter sign. If they will not believe even these two signs or listen to your voice, you shall take some water from the Nile and pour it on the dry ground, and the water that you shall take from the Nile will become blood on the dry ground." (Exodus 4:2–9)

In this passage we read that Moses was told to take various actions, and each time God responded with a supernatural action. The choice for Moses was to obey or disobey. He needed a degree of faith when making the choice, especially when told to pick up the serpent by the tail—normally the worst place to take hold of a snake.

The actions by Moses—and by God—were enough to convince the people that God had sent Moses.

Aaron spoke all the words that the Lord had spoken to Moses and did the signs in the sight of the people. And the people believed ... and they bowed their heads and worshipped. (Exodus 4:30–31)

During the wandering in the wilderness, the Israelites grumbled against Moses and against God, so God sent serpents amongst them.

When the people repented and admitted their sin, God told Moses to erect a bronze serpent on a pole.

> And the Lord said to Moses, "Make a fiery serpent and set it on a pole, and everyone who is bitten, when he sees it, shall live." So Moses made a bronze serpent and set it on a pole. And if a serpent bit anyone, he would look at the bronze serpent and live. (Numbers 21:8–9)

There are several examples of God's sovereignty in action in this incident. The most interesting is this last part. Anyone looking at the serpent on the pole would be cured of the lethal effects of the snake venom. The sovereignty of God is shown in the cure for a lethal condition. The action required appeared to be the looking at the bronze serpent, yet what cured them was the act of faith and obedience which lay behind the looking.

We have a clear parallel here between the serpent on the pole and the Saviour on the cross. We need to look to Him in faith and obedience if we are to live in His presence.

While thinking about Moses, we can see another picture of the coming Christ. To make this clearer, we need to consider a statement by Jesus. As we read in Matthew 16:16, "You are the Christ, the Son of the living God." Jesus answered, "And on this rock I will build my church, and the gates of hell shall not prevail against it" (Matthew 16:18).

When we see Christ as the Rock, the significance of two events in the life of Moses emerges.

When the Israelites were at Horeb, they needed water. God told Moses what to do. Exodus 17:6: "Behold, I will stand before you there on the rock at Horeb, and you shall strike the rock, and water shall come out of it, and the people will drink." And Moses did so, in the sight of the elders of Israel."

Water gushed from the rock, and the need was met in abundance. Here, again, we see an action ordered by God resulting in a response by God in which His sovereignty may be seen.

At a later time, the need for water arose once more. This time God gave Moses a different instruction: "Take the staff, and assemble the congregation, you and Aaron your brother, and tell the rock before their eyes to yield its water. So you shall bring water out of the rock for them and give drink to the congregation and their cattle" (Numbers 20:8).

At this point, Moses disobeyed God.

> And Moses lifted up his hand and struck the rock with his staff twice, and water came out abundantly, and the congregation drank, and their livestock. And the Lord said to Moses and Aaron, "Because you did not believe in me, to uphold me as holy in the eyes of the people of Israel, therefore you shall not bring this assembly into the land that I have given them." (Numbers 20:11–12)

The fact that Moses disobeyed God and struck the rock instead of speaking to it could have resulted in the people's remaining thirsty. However, despite Moses's failing to act correctly, God very graciously met the need for water, abundantly.

God can—and will—work His purposes out through us even when we do take the wrong actions, but we may miss out on some of His blessings as a result.

Because Moses struck this rock, he was not permitted to enter the Promised Land, though he was allowed to see it from a nearby mountain. This punishment seems harsh until we realise that Moses had not simply disobeyed God but also had destroyed the picture which God would have built of His Son. Christ, the Rock, would only need to be struck once. His work on the cross was full and final.

Once was enough. As we read in John 4:14, "Whoever drinks of the water that I will give him will never be thirsty again. The water that I will give him will become in him a spring of water welling up to eternal life."

Jesus has done enough for the salvation of all who look to Him and speak to Him.

Question 25. *If what we do and what we say are not the same, which will people take most notice of, our words or our actions?*

Joshua replaced Moses as leader of the Israelites when they entered the Promised Land. God gave Joshua a great victory over Jericho, but the goods taken from the city were to be kept as an offering to God. As we read in Joshua 6:17, "And the city and all that is within it shall be devoted to the Lord for destruction."

The next battle was against the city of Ai. This turned out to be a disaster. The reader is told the reason for this, but it did not become clear to Joshua until afterwards: "But the people of Israel broke faith in regard to the devoted things, for Achan … took some of the devoted things. And the anger of the Lord burned against the people of Israel" (Joshua 7:1).

Achan had taken some of the plunder which should have been devoted to God and had hidden it in his tent. It was not hidden from God, of course. Achan's action had resulted in defeat for the whole nation and the loss of life of some of its soldiers because the relationship between God and His people had been spoiled.

Another observation here is that God said to Joshua that there was sin in the camp which had to be eradicated before the Israelites would enjoy military success once more. Yet God did not tell Joshua directly who was responsible. This was determined by the random process of casting lots. A process which seems random to us is under the direct control of a sovereign God. Achan was found by the casting of lots, and then the hidden plunder was found.

Like Ananias and Sapphira, Achan died because of a wrong action. But unlike them, he found that stoning was a much less pleasant way to die.

A memorable, but sad, incident in the life of David is defined by a series of actions, yet it started with a failure to act.

We read in 2 Samuel 11:1, "In the spring of the year, the time when kings go out to battle, David sent Joab, and his servants with him, and all Israel. And they ravaged the Ammonites and besieged Rabbah. But David remained at Jerusalem."

We often overlook the fact that David was in Jerusalem when he should have been leading his armies in battle, rather than leaving that to Joab.

Had David acted and taken his army to Rabbah, he would not have been sitting at home on his couch with time on his hands. He would not then have seen Bathsheba from his roof. He would not then have been tempted by his lust for her. As we read in 2 Samuel 11:2, "It happened, late one afternoon, when David arose from his couch and was walking on the roof of the king's house, that he saw from the roof a woman bathing."

It was yielding to the temptation of lust that led David to adultery and the murder of Uriah, Bathsheba's husband, disguised as a military loss.

So, we see here a sad chain of events caused not by an action but by the absence of an action. We can also see that God, in His sovereignty, was still using the decisions of a man to fulfil His own purposes. Bathsheba had been appointed by God to be the mother of Solomon, David's successor to the throne of Israel. She is one of a very few women mentioned—though not actually named—in the genealogy of Jesus, recorded by Matthew: "And David was the father of Solomon by the wife of Uriah" (Matthew 1:6).

Question 26. One error by King David (that of not leading his army to war) led to his adultery. How might small mistakes we make lead us deeper into sin?

There are several occasions in the lives of the prophets where God tells His prophet to take an action as a parable to speak to the people. These actions would be unusual or unexpected, which made them all the more noticeable.

God used these "action parables" in the same way as Jesus used spoken parables—to illustrate a point in a dramatic way which could be understood easily.

Jeremiah was a prophet whose actions were dictated by God in order to warn the people of Jerusalem of the coming destruction of their city which He was intending to bring about as a result of their unfaithfulness to Him.

> Thus says the Lord to me, "Go and buy a linen loincloth and put it round your waist, and do not dip it in water." So I bought a loincloth according to the word of the Lord, and put it round my waist. And the word of the Lord came to me a second time, "Take the loincloth that you have bought, which is round your waist, and arise, go to the Euphrates and hide it there in a cleft of the rock." So I went and hid it by the Euphrates, as the Lord commanded me. And after many days the Lord said to me, "Arise, go to the Euphrates, and take from there the loincloth that I commanded you to hide there." Then I went to the Euphrates, and dug, and I took the loincloth from the place where I had hidden it. And behold, the loincloth was spoiled; it was good for nothing. (Jeremiah 13:1–7)

It is not always the prophet who enacts the parable. Jeremiah was sent by God to watch the actions of a potter, which demonstrated quite forcefully how the sovereign God was able to deal with His people:

> The word that came to Jeremiah from the Lord: "Arise, and go down to the potter's house, and there I will let you hear my words." So I went down to the potter's house, and there he was working at his wheel. And the vessel he was making of clay was spoiled in the potter's hand, and he reworked it into another vessel, as it seemed good to the potter to do. Then the word of the Lord came to me: "O house of Israel, can I not do with you as this potter has done? declares the Lord. Behold, like the clay in the potter's hand, so are you in my hand, O house of Israel." (Jeremiah 18:1–6)

This is a clear picture of God's sovereignty.

Ezekiel was another prophet who acted out some of his message. For example, he demonstrated the overthrow of Judah and the forthcoming captivity:

> As for you, son of man, prepare for yourself an exile's baggage, and go into exile by day in their sight. You shall go like an exile from your place to another place in their sight. Perhaps they will understand, though they are a rebellious house. You shall bring out your baggage by day in their sight, as baggage for exile, and you shall go out yourself at evening in their sight, as those do who must go into exile. (Ezekiel 12:3–4)

God made it clear to Ezekiel that this was symbolism as a warning to Israel of forthcoming exile. As we read in Ezekiel 12:6, "For I have made you a sign for the house of Israel."

The sovereignty of God is underlined in these events. Ezekiel was to tell the people that the message which he had enacted was from the Lord God:

> Son of man, has not the house of Israel, the rebellious house, said to you, "What are you doing?" Say to them, "Thus says the Lord God: This oracle concerns the prince in Jerusalem and all the house of Israel who are in it." Say, "I am a sign for you: as I have done, so shall it be done to them. They shall go into exile, into captivity." (Ezekiel 12:9–11)

God still had a love for His people. He would preserve a remnant who would speak of Him so all nations would know of His sovereignty. As Ezekiel 12:16 reads, "But I will let a few of them escape from the sword, from famine and pestilence, that they may declare all their abominations among the nations where they go, and may know that I am the Lord."

Ezekiel was later given another prophecy which God acted out to him in a dream. We have already seen that the valley of dry bones was a demonstration to Ezekiel of the need for spirituality (chapter 9), yet it was also a demonstration of God's sovereignty. Ezekiel 37:14 reads, "And I will put my Spirit within you, and you shall live, and I will place you in your own land. Then you shall know that I am the Lord; I have spoken, and I will do it, declares the Lord."

After this vision, Ezekiel was given another parable to act out. He was told by God to take two sticks. One stick would represent the southern kingdom of Judah, and the other was to stand for the northern kingdom of Israel. Ezekiel was to hold the two sticks together in one hand to represent the reunification of the nation.

Not only did God make that meaning clear to Ezekiel, but also He asserted, yet again, His sovereignty over His people:

> And I will make them one nation in the land, on the mountains of Israel. And one king shall be king over them all, and they shall be no longer two nations, and no longer divided into two kingdoms. They shall not defile themselves any more with their idols and their detestable things, or with any of their transgressions. But I will save them from all the backsliding in which they have sinned, and will cleanse them; and they shall be my people, and I will be their God. (Ezekiel 37:22–23)

When God determined to deal with the unfaithfulness of His people, he gave them an illustration of that unfaithfulness:

> When the Lord first spoke through Hosea, the Lord said to Hosea, "Go, take to yourself a wife of whoredom and have children of whoredom, for the land commits great whoredom by forsaking the Lord." So he went and took Gomer, the daughter of Diblaim, and she conceived and bore him a son. (Hosea 1:2–3)

We read on that Gomer had not given up her old ways and gave birth to a daughter and a second son who were probably not Hosea's. (The first time, Gomer bore him a son, then she bore a daughter and she bore a son—no "him". The parenting of the second and third children is also questioned in chapter 2 of Hosea.)

The story continues in chapter 3 with Hosea redeeming Gomer at a very significant cost. The cost to God of our redemption was the blood of His Son.

As a contrast to the Old Testament examples, we could look at some cases in the New Testament.

When Jesus and His disciples arrived at Capernaum, the tax collectors asked Peter about Jesus's paying the Temple tax. Jesus, as a rabbi, would not have been required to pay this tax. However, Jesus instructed Peter to pay the tax—and told him where to find the money: "However, not to give offence to them, go to the sea and cast a hook and take the first fish that comes up, and when you open its mouth you will find a shekel. Take that and give it to them for me and for yourself" (Matthew 17:27).

Peter, as a professional fisherman, would normally have used nets, rather than a line, to catch fish. Finding a fish with a coin in its mouth would have been unheard of, and he only needed to catch a single fish to find the coin. The coin was the exact amount needed for the tax for two people: Jesus and Peter.

Peter had to act to find the coin. This would not have been normal practice for finding money. We are not told how the coin came to be in the mouth of the fish, but God, in His sovereignty, had everything in place. Peter had only to act as he had been told, and then all was well.

Another incident involving fish occurred soon after the resurrection of Jesus. The disciples had been fishing unsuccessfully all night. The appearance of Jesus in the morning made a great difference to them. Jesus simply told them to do something which would have seemed totally pointless to them, especially as they had not recognised Jesus by then.

> Jesus said to them, "Children, do you have any fish?" They
> answered him, "No." He said to them, "Cast the net on the
> right side of the boat, and you will find some." So they cast
> it, and now they were not able to haul it in, because of the
> quantity of fish. (John 18:33-38)

The action required by the disciples was simple: casting the net on the other side of the boat. Their reward was a large haul of fish, which showed, once more, that the sovereign God has mastery over His creation.

We saw in the previous chapter that the story of Onesimus helps us explore the relationship between people. It also shows the relationship between our actions and God's sovereignty, in two ways. Firstly, we see a slave who has acted in a wrong way, yet God was in control of him. Onesimus had run away from his master, Philemon, and God had directed him to Paul, where he had heard the gospel and become a Christian.

Philemon 10 reads, "I appeal to you for my child, Onesimus, whose father I became in my imprisonment." So we see God, in His sovereignty, using the action of a sinful man for His own glory.

Secondly, we have an example in Paul of the way in which the sovereign God often works:

> Accordingly, though I am bold enough in Christ to command you to do what is required, yet for love's sake I prefer to appeal to you—I, Paul, an old man and now a prisoner also for Christ Jesus—I appeal to you for my child, Onesimus. (Philemon 8–10)

Here, Paul is saying that he wanted Philemon to choose to take the right action rather than Paul's telling him that he must. If we are to please God, we will choose to do the right thing, not wait until we miss out on a blessing because God compels us to act or brings His will about some other way.

One final thought here. There was one crucial act which was part of a series of actions which turned history on its head. As Jesus stood before Pilate, Pilate asked if Jesus was the King of the Jews. Jesus replied that His kingdom was not of this world. When pressed on the point, He gave an answer to Pilate which would have been taken as blasphemy, though from Jesus it was the truth.

> So Pilate entered his headquarters again and called Jesus and said to him, "Are you the King of the Jews?" Jesus answered, "Do you say this of your own accord, or did others say it to you about me?" Pilate answered, "Am I a

Jew? Your own nation and the chief priests have delivered you over to me. What have you done?" Jesus answered, "My kingdom is not of this world. If my kingdom were of this world, my servants would have been fighting, that I might not be delivered over to the Jews. But my kingdom is not from the world." Then Pilate said to him, "So you are a king?" Jesus answered, "You say that I am a king. For this purpose I was born and for this purpose I have come into the world—to bear witness to the truth. Everyone who is of the truth listens to my voice." Pilate said to him, "What is truth?" (John 18:33–38)

The actions of Jesus in Jerusalem led to His crucifixion. This was the greatest part of God's sovereign plan, which He made known from the beginning.

We read in Genesis 3:15, "I will put enmity between you and the woman, and between your offspring and her offspring; he shall bruise your head, and you shall bruise his heel."

THE SOVEREIGNTY OF GOD IN MANAGEMENT

Suggested Background Reading: 1 Timothy 5

P aul was a great believer in order in church life. Whilst the thrust of his letters was usually about doctrine, he frequently slipped in comments about how worship should be conducted and how Christians should behave within church and outside.

The church in Corinth was surrounded by a culture of deplorable attitudes towards life in general and by sexual misconduct in particular. Unfortunately, the attitudes of the world had started to infiltrate the church. The letters which Paul wrote to the pastor of the church in Ephesus contain stern warnings about the results of failure to resist and to reverse that trend. We have two of these letters in our scriptures. From these, we can learn a great deal about church management.

Timothy was a man for whom Paul had a great deal of respect. Timothy became the pastor of the church in Ephesus at a relatively young age. Paul wrote at least two letters to him, giving him fatherly advice on church management. These letters are softer in tone than those sent to (for example) Corinth. Paul also wrote a letter of pastoral advice to Titus, which we have available.

Pauls' concern was that life in church, as well as the life of Christians in general, should be honouring to God.

As we have seen before, God chose to impose His sovereign will on the churches not by direct intervention but by inspiring Paul to write down what His will was for the churches and to send it to them. This means not only that God was not treating His people as robots but also means that we may read the documents ourselves and understand how we should manage church life today.

Two of the most useful comments we have on this issue are found in the same chapter of one of the letters to Corinth. They give the fundamental purpose of church life and the test for the suitability of any particular activity: "Let all things be done for building up. … All things should be done decently and in order" (1 Corinthians 14:26, 40).

The spur to action from all this should be to ask ourselves how God would have us behave if He were to force us to act like robots—and then to do that anyway as an act of love, worship, and devotion.

With this in mind, we look to see how we should manage our affairs, including church life, in a way which is in line with the will of a sovereign God.

Most of Paul's advice to Timothy about church management related to his dealings with people.

In the early days of the church, there were problems arising from the growing need for practical support alongside the spiritual work. The same men were struggling to cope with the demands, so helpers were appointed take on the tasks such as food distribution to those in need, leaving the apostles to concentrate on the spiritual work.

Acts 6:2–4 reads, "It is not right that we should give up preaching the word of God to serve tables. Therefore, brothers, pick out from among you seven men of good repute, full of the Spirit and of wisdom, whom we will appoint to this duty. But we will devote ourselves to prayer and to the ministry of the word."

This developed into a pattern of church leadership which is still used in many churches today. It consists of a pastor as spiritual leader, under God, working with elders to teach and nurture the congregation. Then there are deacons concerned with the day-to- day running of the church so as not to distract from the worship and preaching.

Paul told Timothy and Titus what sort of men should be chosen for these roles. Paul is saying that this responsibility was to be held by responsible men:

> Therefore an overseer must be above reproach, the husband of one wife, sober-minded, self-controlled, respectable, hospitable, able to teach, not a drunkard, not violent but gentle, not quarrelsome, not a lover of money. He must manage his own household well, with all dignity keeping his children submissive, for if someone does not know how to manage his own household, how will he care for God's church? He must not be a recent convert, or he may become puffed up with conceit and fall into the condemnation of the devil. Moreover, he must be well thought of by outsiders, so that he may not fall into disgrace, into a snare of the devil. (1 Timothy 3:2–7)

The requirements for deacons appear to be remarkably similar:

> Deacons likewise must be dignified, not double-tongued, not addicted to much wine, not greedy for dishonest gain. They must hold the mystery of the faith with a clear conscience. And let them also be tested first; then let them serve as deacons if they prove themselves blameless.

> Their wives likewise must be dignified, not slanderers, but sober-minded, faithful in all things. Let deacons each be the husband of one wife, managing their children and their own households well. For those who serve well as deacons gain a good standing for themselves and also great confidence in the faith that is in Christ Jesus. (1 Timothy 3:8–13)

When Paul wrote to Titus, he cited similar characteristics, but Paul had told him of the need to appoint elders. These were not needed only in Jerusalem but in every town.

> This is why I left you in Crete, so that you might put what remained into order, and appoint elders in every town as I directed you—if anyone is above reproach, the husband of one wife, and his children are believers and not open to the charge of debauchery or insubordination. For an overseer, as God's steward, must be above reproach. He must not be arrogant or quick-tempered or a drunkard or violent or greedy for gain, but hospitable, a lover of good, self-controlled, upright, holy, and disciplined. He must hold firm to the trustworthy word as taught, so that he may be able to give instruction in sound doctrine and also to rebuke those who contradict it. (Titus 1:5–9)

The requirement that elders and deacons should be men who are able to manage their own households well is no accident. Paul asked the question "For if someone does not know how to manage his own household, how will he care for God's church?" Positions of responsibility were to be held by those whose spirituality and general lifestyle was worthy of the name of Christ, but also it was required that they have the skills needed to do an effective job of managing the church.

Timothy is also reminded of the need to honour those elders who serve well, and also of the scriptural basis for this:

> Let the elders who rule well be considered worthy of double honour, especially those who labour in preaching and teaching. For the Scripture says, "You shall not muzzle an ox when it treads out the grain" [Deuteronomy 25:4] and, "The labourer deserves his wages [Matthew 10:10; Luke 10:7]." (1 Timothy 5:17–18)

In some churches, deacons are seen as inferior to elders, but if the standards required are the same, then surely they are equal in God's eyes. We could go further and say that these requirements are what God seeks from each one of His children.

The details of how elders and deacons are appointed may vary from church to church, but in each case, God will have His hand on those who make the decisions so that they are appointed by God's sovereignty.

There was a church in London some years ago which had a leadership team consisting of five elders and one deacon. They worked as a team of six with no distinction between the deacon and the others. When we asked why they were not all called elders, we were told that the one man could not be an elder since he was single and not, therefore, the husband of one wife. This is meaningless in view of the marriage comment applying to deacons too. In fact, Paul was saying that church leaders should not be bigamists, not that they must be married. The main point is, of course, that those who are in a position of responsibility in a church should live a life which is worthy of the name of Christ and be able to undertake the tasks assigned to them.

Question 27. *The qualities needed for someone to be a church leader are very high. Can anybody be a church leader?*

Paul had more to say about the way that God would like to have His churches managed. Paul reminded Timothy that people should be treated with respect:

> Do not rebuke an older man but encourage him as you
> would a father, younger men as brothers, older women as
> mothers, younger women as sisters, in all purity. Honour
> widows who are truly widows. (1 Timothy 5:1–3)

He also stressed the need for those who can be supported by their
families to use that support to prevent the church from being overloaded:

> If any believing woman has relatives who are widows, let
> her care for them. Let the church not be burdened, so that it
> may care for those who are truly widows. (1 Timothy 5:16)

Church discipline is a difficult subject to talk about in some churches.
Paul is quite clear that problems in the church have to be dealt with
correctly:

> Do not admit a charge against an elder except on the
> evidence of two or three witnesses. As for those who persist
> in sin, rebuke them in the presence of all, so that the rest
> may stand in fear. In the presence of God and of Christ
> Jesus and of the elect angels I charge you to keep these
> rules without prejudging, doing nothing from partiality.
> (1 Timothy 5:19–21)

The world is watching (so is God)!

> The sins of some men are conspicuous, going before them
> to judgement, but the sins of others appear later. So also
> good works are conspicuous, and even those that are not
> cannot remain hidden. (1 Timothy 5:24–25)

The management of God's people became an issue long before the
events of the New Testament and the start of the Christian church.

Moses had problems as leader of the Israelites because the size of the
nation became so large that he could not cope with the number of

demands on his time and attention or with the level of criticism and moaning against him—and against God—because the people had no meat to eat in the wilderness. Moses says in Numbers 11:14, "I am not able to carry all this people alone; the burden is too heavy for me."

Wisely, Moses turned to God for a solution to the problem. The sovereign God had His answer ready and waiting:

> Then the Lord said to Moses, "Gather for me seventy men of the elders of Israel, whom you know to be the elders of the people and officers over them, and bring them to the tent of meeting, and let them take their stand there with you. And I will come down and talk with you there. And I will take some of the Spirit that is on you and put it on them, and they shall bear the burden of the people with you, so that you may not bear it yourself alone." (Numbers 11:16–17)

Moses's obedience resulted in God's providing a significant degree of support for him in the management of the Israelites, but it also resulted in a dramatic sign that Moses had the Spirit of God on him and that this Spirit was also on the seventy elders appointed to help him.

> So Moses went out and told the people the words of the Lord. And he gathered seventy men of the elders of the people and placed them round the tent. Then the Lord came down in the cloud and spoke to him, and took some of the Spirit that was on him and put it on the seventy elders. And as soon as the Spirit rested on them, they prophesied. But they did not continue doing it. (Numbers 11:24–25)

Another time that Moses was given instructions to help in the management of the people was when he was told to take a census of the men who were potential military personnel.

> The Lord spoke to Moses in the wilderness of Sinai, in the tent of meeting, on the first day of the second month,

in the second year after they had come out of the land of Egypt, saying, "Take a census of all the congregation of the people of Israel, by clans, by fathers' houses, according to the number of names, every male, head by head. From twenty years old and upwards, all in Israel who are able to go to war, you and Aaron shall list them, company by company. And there shall be with you a man from each tribe, each man being the head of the house of his fathers." (Numbers 1:1–4)

Not only had God determined that Moses should know how many fighting men he had, but also He provided Moses with a way of managing the census. Counting over six hundred thousand men by himself would have been impossible, so God stipulated one man from each tribe who was to organise the census for that tribe.

This also gives us some idea of the size of the nation being led by Moses. The number does not include boys under the age of twenty, girls or women of any age, or Levites (who were exempt from military duties to enable them to take care of the tabernacle).

Going back even further in time, we find God putting a management structure in place for a situation which had not yet arisen.

To start with, God needed His man, Joseph, in Egypt. He did this by arousing the jealousy of Joseph's brothers and their greed for money.

Then Judah said to his brothers, "What profit is it if we kill our brother and conceal his blood? Come, let us sell him to the Ishmaelites, and let not our hand be upon him, for he is our brother, our own flesh." And his brothers listened to him. Then Midianite traders passed by. And they drew Joseph up and lifted him out of the pit, and sold him to the Ishmaelites for twenty shekels of silver. They took Joseph to Egypt. (Genesis 37:26–28)

Because of false accusations by the wife of Potiphar, Joseph's Egyptian master, Joseph was put in prison. This was all part of God's plan to place Joseph where He needed him.

> And the keeper of the prison put Joseph in charge of all the prisoners who were in the prison. Whatever was done there, he was the one who did it. The keeper of the prison paid no attention to anything that was in Joseph's charge, because the Lord was with him. And whatever he did, the Lord made it succeed. (Genesis 39:22–23)

The next stage in God's plan was for two of Pharaoh's servants to be put into the same prison as Joseph. Here they became aware of Joseph's ability—through God—to interpret dreams.

> They said to him, "We have had dreams, and there is no one to interpret them." And Joseph said to them, "Do not interpretations belong to God? Please tell them to me." (Genesis 40:8)

So it was when Pharaoh had a dream that his cup-bearer remembered Joseph and told Pharaoh about his ability to interpret dreams. God then used Joseph to interpret a dream which He had given Pharaoh:

> It is as I told Pharaoh; God has shown to Pharaoh what he is about to do. There will come seven years of great plenty throughout all the land of Egypt, but after them there will arise seven years of famine, and all the plenty will be forgotten in the land of Egypt. The famine will consume the land. (Genesis 41:28–30)

The scene was now set for Joseph to manage the food in Egypt over the following fourteen years.

We can be in no doubt that all of this was within the sovereign will of God as it prepared the way for Jacob to move to Egypt to escape famine, for his family to settle there, and for Moses to bring the Israelites out of Egypt. The prophet Hosea helps us to link this with God's greatest act of sovereignty: "When Israel was a child, I loved him, and out of Egypt I called my son" (Hosea 11:1).

So the real drama of these events is that it shows us the pattern for the coming of Jesus in person, many years later. On that occasion, an angel spoke to another Joseph, also by a dream, sending him to Egypt so that the prophecy of Hosea would finally be fulfilled:

> Now when they [the Wise Men] had departed, behold, an angel of the Lord appeared to Joseph in a dream and said, "Rise, take the child and his mother, and flee to Egypt, and remain there until I tell you, for Herod is about to search for the child, to destroy him." And he rose and took the child and his mother by night and departed to Egypt and remained there until the death of Herod. This was to fulfil what the Lord had spoken by the prophet, "Out of Egypt I called my son." (Matthew 2:13–15)

Elijah was another of God's people who was affected by famine, and he, like Joseph, warned the king that it was coming: "Now Elijah the Tishbite, of Tishbe in Gilead, said to Ahab, 'As the Lord, the God of Israel, lives, before whom I stand, there shall be neither dew nor rain these years, except by my word'" (1 Kings 17:1).

In Egypt, God had prepared His man Joseph to manage the situation. In Israel, years later, He had prepared for Elijah to be provided for using His creatures—ravens.

> "You shall drink from the brook, and I have commanded the ravens to feed you there." So [Elijah] went and did according to the word of the Lord. He went and lived by the brook Cherith that is east of the Jordan. And the ravens brought him bread and meat in the morning, and bread and meat in the evening, and he drank from the brook. (1 Kings 17:4–6)

These verses, by themselves, leave us in no doubt about the sovereignty of God. Wild birds will do their best to keep well away from humans. For these birds to be bringing food to Elijah at all is, therefore, quite extraordinary, but for this to happen at a time of food shortage truly is a miracle.

God's sovereignty over nature is further demonstrated in the events which followed. The brook Cherith eventually dried up, but God had other plans to manage Elijah's well-being:

> Then the word of the Lord came to him, "Arise, go to Zarephath, which belongs to Sidon, and dwell there. Behold, I have commanded a widow there to feed you." (1 Kings 17:8–9)

At first this seemed as if everything had gone wrong. The woman and her son were about to eat their last meagre meal before dying of starvation. The woman had to act out her faith in God to discover that His provision for Elijah was afforded to her too. Living by faith in God is a major theme of the Bible.

> "For thus says the Lord, the God of Israel, 'The jar of flour shall not be spent, and the jug of oil shall not be empty, until the day that the Lord sends rain upon the earth.'" And she went and did as Elijah said. And she and he and her household ate for many days. The jar of flour was not spent, neither did the jug of oil become empty, according to the word of the Lord that he spoke by Elijah. (1 Kings 17:14–16)

Solomon is renowned for his wisdom. His management skills were needed for the affairs of state and also for the major undertaking of the building of the Temple. One might suppose that considerable skill would be needed to manage seven hundred wives and three hundred concubines!

When God offered Solomon a gift to help his monarchy, instead of choosing fame or fortune, Solomon asked for wisdom. In a sense he was asking for management skills.

> At Gibeon the Lord appeared to Solomon in a dream by night, and God said, "Ask what I shall give you." And Solomon said, "You have shown great and steadfast love to your servant David my father, because he walked before you in faithfulness, in righteousness, and in uprightness of heart towards you. And you have kept for him this great and steadfast love and have given him a son to sit on his throne this day. ... Give your servant therefore an understanding mind to govern your people, that I may discern between good and evil, for who is able to govern this your great people?" (1 Kings 3:5–6, 9)

Not only did God give Solomon the wisdom for which he asked, but also He gave him great fame and wealth. Solomon's wealth and fame have been well-documented in scripture, where we also have an example of Solomon's skill at managing a legal situation:

> Then two prostitutes came to the king and stood before him. ... Then the king said, "One says, 'This is my son that is alive, and your son is dead'; and the other says, 'No; but your son is dead, and my son is the living one.'" And the king said, "Bring me a sword." So a sword was brought before the king. And the king said, "Divide the living child in two, and give half to one and half to the other." Then the woman whose son was alive said to the king, because her heart yearned for her son, "Oh, my lord, give her the living child, and by no means put him to death." But the other said, "He shall be neither mine nor yours; divide him." Then the king answered and said, "Give the living child to the first woman, and by no means put him to death; she is his mother." (1 Kings 3:16, 23–27)

It is a sad fact that Solomon's management skills did not extend to his harem. The foreign wives may have helped Solomon to have a reign which was largely peaceful, but the women turned him away from God.

> Solomon clung to these [foreign women] in love. He had 700 wives, princesses, and 300 concubines. And his wives turned away his heart. For when Solomon was old his wives turned away his heart after other gods, and his heart was not wholly true to the Lord his God, as was the heart of David his father. (1 Kings 11:2–4)

Question 28: *Solomon, the wisest man who ever lived, allowed his wives to turn him away from worshipping God. What steps should we take to keep ourselves from being turned away?*

God has also ordained that many of the tasks He gives us in His service are undertaken more easily when managed in a structured way. Many of us meet situations like this quite frequently. When we do so, it may help to look at another case where God's work—and therefore His will—was completed more efficiently by the use of a systematic approach.

Nehemiah had been entrusted by God to rebuild Jerusalem, starting with the walls. Nehemiah achieved this vast undertaking by dividing his workers up and giving each group a section of the wall.

> Then Eliashib the high priest rose up with his brothers the priests, and they built the Sheep Gate. They consecrated it and set up its doors. They consecrated it as far as the Tower of the Hundred, as far as the Tower of Hananel. And next to him the men of Jericho built. And next to them Zaccur the son of Imri built. (Nehemiah 3:1–2)

The whole of this chapter tells of who was building each section of the wall.

And between the upper chamber of the corner and the
Sheep Gate the goldsmiths and the merchants repaired.
(Nehemiah 3:32)

The list of workers starts at the Sheep Gate and goes round the city in
order as far as the Sheep Gate. In other words, every part of the wall
had somebody allocated to repair it.

Finally, we might notice that Jesus used management skills when
sending His disciples out before Him:

And he called the twelve and began to send them out two
by two, and gave them authority over the unclean spirits.
… And they cast out many demons and anointed with oil
many who were sick and healed them. (Mark 6:7, 13)

THE SOVEREIGNTY OF GOD IN PRAYER

Suggested Background Reading: John 17,
Matthew 26:36–46, and Acts 4:23–31

B efore considering the topic of prayer, it would be helpful to make sure that we understand what prayer is or, more to the point, what it is not. It is possible to buy books of prayers and read them as ordinary poetry. Reading a prayer can be very enjoyable. Especially if picturesque language is used, it can be very comforting, very stimulating, or even very challenging, but this is not, in itself, praying. Saying a prayer is not praying. Saying or reading a prayer is an exercise of the mind only. Prayer must come from the heart. It is possible to pray a prayer while reading it, but the reality is that too often the words are not made into our own conversation with God, or else they lack any sincerity.

We should also be careful to blur the distinction between prayers of praise and worship on one hand and intercessory prayer on the other.

In the High Priestly Prayer of Jesus, recorded by John (chapter 17), we see Jesus praying some very significant words. In verse 11 we read, "And I am coming to you. Holy Father, keep them in your name,

which you have given me, that they may be one, even as we are one."
While in verse 24 He says, "Father, I desire that they also, whom you
have given me, may be with me where I am, to see my glory that you
have given me because you loved me before the foundation of the
world."

It may seem surprising that Jesus should pray such words to His Father
when He had already told His disciples that those who trusted in Him
would be with Him in His glory.

> All that the Father gives me will come to me, and whoever
> comes to me I will never cast out. For I have come down
> from heaven, not to do my own will but the will of him
> who sent me. And this is the will of him who sent me, that
> I should lose nothing of all that he has given me, but raise
> it up on the last day. For this is the will of my Father, that
> everyone who looks on the Son and believes in him should
> have eternal life, and I will raise him up on the last day.
> (John 6:37–40)

This passage makes it quite clear that Jesus knew, before He prayed
for the protection of those whom God had given Him, that we would,
indeed, already be under God's protection. The last verse makes it
equally clear that Jesus knew that this was the will of God. Jesus is
effectively saying to God, "I know that You want to do this, and I
know that You are going to do this, so please do it!"

This should set the pattern for our intercessory prayer to a sovereign
God.

Prayer should not be a formality or a routine activity where we try to
change God's will, but a humble submission of our will to Him. As
Søren Kierkegaard put it, "Prayer does not change God, but it changes
those who pray." When Jesus says that we can ask for anything and
be sure of receiving it, He adds a very important qualification—"if
you ask in My name".

> Truly, truly, I say to you, whatever you ask of the Father in
> my name, he will give it to you. Until now you have asked
> nothing in my name. Ask, and you will receive, that your
> joy may be full. (John 16:23–24)

Think here of a father holding a gift for his son. He has determined to give him the gift, and he knows the gift will be good for him, but he waits for him to ask before giving it to him. Our heavenly Father has good gifts for us, but He often waits for us to ask for them. If we ask in Jesus's name, this is not just a phrase to put at the end of a prayer as a kind of magic formula so that God has to answer us. Rather, it is a sign that we have aligned our wills to His, having asked only for things that Jesus would have asked for.

Praying within the will of God is essential because we are not capable of directing our own paths aright. It is purely the Lord who establishes our steps. As we read in Jeremiah 10:23, "I know, O Lord, that the way of man is not in himself, that it is not in man who walks to direct his steps."

Proverbs 16:9 tells us, "The heart of man plans his way, but the Lord establishes his steps."

For us to attempt to suggest that the sovereign God should change His will or His plans in any way just because we ask Him to would be arrogance of the highest order. We cannot understand His purposes, which may involve things which we find difficult, yet His plans will have ends which are for our eternal good. As Romans 8:28 tells us, "And we know that for those who love God all things work together for good, for those who are called according to his purpose."

Thus we should not lose sight of the fact that prayer is a humble acknowledgement of our dependence on a sovereign God. Any emphasis on the human aspect of prayer, rather than the divine side, is to be avoided at all costs.

There are those who teach that God, in His sovereignty, has ordained that human destinies may be changed and moulded by the will of humankind. This cannot be true when God has His plans for each of us and when these plans are the best for us. God, in His sovereignty, ensures that His plans are carried out. God does not change His will because we pray. What prayer changes is our relationship with God.

The ultimate destiny of a person is determined by where he or she stands before God, whether or not he or she has been born again. This is quite clear in scripture, both the Old Testament and the New Testament.

> The Lord kills and brings to life; he brings down to Sheol and raises up. The Lord makes poor and makes rich; he brings low and he exalts. He raises up the poor from the dust; he lifts the needy from the ash heap to make them sit with princes and inherit a seat of honour. For the pillars of the earth are the Lord's, and on them he has set the world. (1 Samuel 2:6–8)

> But to all who did receive him, who believed in his name, he gave the right to become children of God, who were born, not of blood nor of the will of the flesh nor of the will of man, but of God. (John 1:12–13)

> Jesus answered [Nicodemus], "Truly, truly, I say to you, unless one is born of water and the Spirit, he cannot enter the kingdom of God." (John 3:5)

Some years ago, the editor of a religious weekly journal quoted an unnamed source as saying, "There are certain things that will happen in a man's life whether he prays or not. There are other things that will happen if he prays, and will not happen if he does not pray."

The first part of this statement is obviously true in the life of anyone who never prays. When a believer prays "Your will be done", he or she can be sure that it will be. What is lost by failure to pray, however, is not any sort of event or fulfilment of God's plans, but a lack of an effective relationship with God.

The same editorial included the story of a Christian worker who was impressed by the content of the unnamed source. As he entered a business office, he prayed that the Lord would open the way for him to speak to someone about Christ, reflecting that things would be changed when he prayed. Then his mind turned to other things and the prayer was forgotten. The opportunity came to speak to the businessman on whom he was calling, but he did not grasp it. He was on his way out when he remembered his prayer of half an hour before and God's answer. He promptly returned and had a talk with the businessman, who, though a church member, had never in his life been asked whether he was saved.

The late A. W. Pink, in his work *The Sovereignty of God*, comments on this account:

> The example [of the Christian worker and the businessman] is a very unhappy one. According to the terms of the illustration, the Christian worker's prayer is not answered by God at all, inasmuch as, apparently, the way was not opened to speak to the businessman about his soul. But on leaving the office and recalling his prayer, the Christian worker (perhaps in the energy of the flesh) determined to answer the prayer for himself, and instead of leaving the Lord to "open the way" for him, took matters into his own hand.

This criticism seems to be a little harsh. A Christian should be seeking an opportunity to speak for Christ all the time. The prayer of this Christian worker suggests that he was aware of this and wanted to be in the service of God. On the face of it he missed the opportunity to speak up during the meeting. The calling to mind of the prayer as he left may have been the result of an intervention by the Holy

Spirit, who determined that the businessman would be more amenable to considering his spiritual state without the pressure of discussing business at the same time.

Another (anonymous) quote from a book states, "The possibilities and necessity of prayer, its power and results, are manifested in arresting and changing the purposes of God and in relieving the stroke of His power."

The scriptures tell us quite clearly that we can never arrest or change the purposes of God. If we think otherwise, we are denying the sovereignty of God and are deceiving ourselves.

> For his dominion is an everlasting dominion, and his kingdom endures from generation to generation; all the inhabitants of the earth are accounted as nothing, and he does according to his will among the host of heaven and among the inhabitants of the earth; and none can stay his hand or say to him, "What have you done?" (Daniel 4:34–35)

We can see that it is even more serious to think that we can change God's eternal purposes when we realise that, in so doing, we are claiming that our purposes are superior to His and that His purposes, laid down before time began, are in some way faulty. We often have occasion to alter our plans because we make them without knowing all the possible outcomes or the circumstances in which we'll have to operate. Things around us may change either before we execute our plans or while we are doing so, and then we have to adapt what we are doing. The eternal God has plans which are built around His knowledge of every detail and of every outcome. His plans are perfect and never need to be adapted or modified.

The *Sovereignty of God*, quoted above, also contains the following:

> The prayers of God's saints are the capital stock in heaven
> by which Christ carries on His great work upon earth.

> The great throes and mighty convulsions on earth are the
> results of these prayers. Earth is changed, revolutionized,
> angels move on more powerful, rapid wing, and God's
> policy is shaped as the prayers are more numerous, more
> efficient.

Once again, this suggests that God is making things up as He goes along and that He is looking to His people on earth to tell Him what to do next. This is a total denial of the sovereignty of God and His eternal purposes. Paul tells us quite openly that God's purposes are eternal and that He works all things according to the counsel of His will:

> The plan of the mystery hidden for ages in God who
> created all things, so that through the church the manifold
> wisdom of God might now be made known to the rulers
> and authorities in the heavenly places. This was according
> to the eternal purpose that he has realised in Christ Jesus
> our Lord. (Ephesians 3:9–11)

> In him we have obtained an inheritance, having been
> predestined according to the purpose of him who works all
> things according to the counsel of his will. (Ephesians 1:11)

Since God's purposes are eternal, there is no way in which we can change them, either through prayer or in any other way. All we can do is to submit our wills to that of our Creator.

> Oh, the depth of the riches and wisdom and knowledge
> of God! How unsearchable are his judgements and how
> inscrutable his ways! For who has known the mind of the
> Lord, or who has been his counsellor? (Romans 11:33–34)

Question 29. *What are the main differences between "praying" and "saying prayers"? Which of these categories would "reading prayers" fall into?*

The truth which lies behind all this discussion is that we have a very great and mighty God. We are confident that our faith in Him is well placed because of His sovereignty. If God could not be relied on to be unchanging, then there would be little point in praying to Him in any event. If we were to pray for a particular outcome of an event and if God then agreed to make it happen, could we be satisfied that nobody else would seek God for a different outcome to that event, resulting in God changing His mind?

Had we the ability to change God's mind, then we would also have serious conflict between ourselves.

Consider the man whose garden is in need of water, so he prays for rain. His neighbour, who has taken a day's leave from work in order to paint his garden shed, prays that it will not rain. Which prayer would God answer? Then there might be a situation where two Christians are about to compete in a race and both pray that God will help them win. Will the winner be the one who can pray better or the one who can run faster?

In these cases, we can see that at least one of those praying would not be praying within God's will, as Jesus prayed to His Father: "Not as I will, but as you will" (Matthew 26:39).

These principles can be best summed up in a comment by Martin Luther: "Prayer is not overcoming God's reluctance, but laying hold of His willingness."

Far too many of our prayer meetings consist of our coming to God with a "shopping list" of requests. We try to use prayer as a "slot machine" where we put our prayer in and expect God to put the answer out automatically. This is dishonouring to God. It also shows a misunderstanding of what prayer is all about.

This seems a rather negative approach thus far. So, having looked at what prayer is not, let us turn our attention to what it is.

Our primary purpose in prayer must be to praise God for who He is. As we read in Isaiah 57:15, "For thus says the One who is high and lifted up, who inhabits eternity, whose name is Holy: 'I dwell in the high and holy place.'"

To acknowledge God as the Sovereign of the universe is to make the statement that we are presenting ourselves before the One who has the power to work in our lives and the power to save us from our sinfulness.

Jonah was a man who blatantly and openly disobeyed the Lord. God told him to go north-east, but he immediately headed south-west. As he sought to flee from the presence of God, God intervened and stopped him by a storm at sea. Jonah found himself inside a great fish, where he considered his position and called out to God in prayer. His prayer was not "Please get me out of this fish" but was a prayer of penitence and submission to God, ending with an amazing statement in which he recognised God's power: "Salvation belongs to the Lord!" (Jonah 2:9).

Hand in hand with praising God for who He is will be our worship of Him and our expression of our love for Him, reflecting, albeit in a poor way, His great love for us. Our worship of God is our expression of His "worth-ship" as we lay it before a good, powerful, unchanging, gracious sovereign God.

Also, as we pray, we are glorifying God. There are no better examples of this than in the High Priestly Prayer of Jesus and prayers being uttered in the very throne room of God in heaven:

> When Jesus had spoken these words, he lifted up his eyes to heaven, and said, "Father, the hour has come; glorify your Son that the Son may glorify you, since you have given him authority over all flesh, to give eternal life to all whom you have given him. And this is eternal life, that they know you the only true God, and Jesus Christ whom you have sent. I

glorified you on earth, having accomplished the work that you gave me to do. And now, Father, glorify me in your own presence with the glory that I had with you before the world existed." (John 17:1–5)

"Worthy is the Lamb who was slain, to receive power and wealth and wisdom and might and honour and glory and blessing!" And I heard every creature in heaven and on earth and under the earth and in the sea, and all that is in them, saying, "To him who sits on the throne and to the Lamb be blessing and honour and glory and might for ever and ever!" (Revelation 5:12–13)

Amen! Blessing and glory and wisdom and thanksgiving and honour and power and might be to our God for ever and ever! Amen. (Revelation 7:12)

Praying like this, we are constantly being reminded of God's greatness and our place before Him. Prayer is an act of humility.

Prayer is also given to us for our own benefit. God is pleased to pour spiritual blessings upon us as we spend time in His presence. It is through prayer that we grow in grace and are drawn closer to Him. We normally think of God speaking to us as we read His Word, which He often does, but He also may speak to us as we bow before Him in prayer. Romans 10:17 reads, "So faith comes from hearing, and hearing through the word of Christ."

Compare this with the conversation between Abraham and the Lord. Abraham is speaking to the Lord in prayer, and the Lord is answering him as he does so:

Abraham still stood before the Lord. Then Abraham drew near and said, "Will you indeed sweep away the righteous with the wicked? Suppose there are fifty righteous within the city. Will you then sweep away the place and not spare

> it for the fifty righteous who are in it? Far be it from you to do such a thing, to put the righteous to death with the wicked, so that the righteous fare as the wicked! Far be that from you! Shall not the Judge of all the earth do what is just?" And the Lord said, "If I find at Sodom fifty righteous in the city, I will spare the whole place for their sake." (Genesis 18:22–26)

We also know that God spoke to Jesus as He was praying within the hearing of a crowd of people: "Father, glorify your name." Then a voice came from heaven: "I have glorified it, and I will glorify it again" (John 12:28).

Another important component of prayer is our expression of love, which is strengthened by the very act of praying, as the psalmist points out: "I love the Lord, because he has heard my voice and my pleas for mercy" (Psalm 116:1).

Question 30. *Why do we need to pray to a sovereign God who will act according to His divine purpose anyway?*

When we have brought our praise, our worship, and our thanksgiving, we are then in a position to make supplication to God for the things which we need from Him. Here we need to be more careful to pray within the sovereign will of God. Of course, He already knows of our needs, even better than we do, but in coming to Him, we are laying our needs before Him and humbly expressing our total dependence on Him for all the blessings He gives us.

This underlines the fact that our asking God for what He already knows we need is not a meaningless exercise. We are called upon to pray and give thanks because this is the will of God and because it brings us encouragement. We read in 1 Thessalonians 5:17–18, "Pray without ceasing, give thanks in all circumstances; for this is the will of God in Christ Jesus for you."

Luke 18:1 tells us, "And he told them a parable to the effect that they ought always to pray and not lose heart."

James reminds us that our prayer is linked to our righteousness and should be underpinned by our faith:

> And the prayer of faith will save the one who is sick, and the Lord will raise him up. And if he has committed sins, he will be forgiven. Therefore, confess your sins to one another and pray for one another, that you may be healed. The effective prayer of a righteous person has great power. (James 5:15–16)

Jesus also talks about the need for faith when praying. "If you have faith like a grain of mustard seed, you will say to this mountain, 'Move from here to there,' and it will move, and nothing will be impossible for you" (Matthew 17:20).

There is a story of a woman who bought a new house. One day she realised that there would be a terrific view from the bedroom window if a hill were not there. She knew about faith to move mountains, so that night she prayed that God would move the hill out of the way of her view. When she woke up in the morning, she rushed to the window and threw back the curtains. To her disappointment, the hill was still there. "Well," she said, "I thought it would be!"

This shows not only that the woman was lacking in faith but also that there is, surely, another reason why her prayer was not answered. James 4:2–3 spells this out very clearly: "You do not have, because you do not ask. You ask and do not receive, because you ask wrongly, to spend it on your passions."

Prayer for the sake of greed is not the same as prayer in the will of God.

Compare this with another story, about a little girl who lived in Wales. There was a great drought which was causing a lot of distress. Supplies of water were becoming very low, crops were dying, and animals were struggling to find water to drink. Everyone was suffering from the heat. The villagers from a badly hit area decided to hold a prayer meeting to plead for God to send rain. As they assembled in the church, all wearing the most summery of clothes, the little girl turned up carrying an umbrella. Several folks poked fun at her. "We have had no rain for four weeks, it's a scorching hot day, and there's not a cloud in the sky. Why are you carrying that umbrella?" Her answer was simple and to the point: "We're coming to pray for rain!" She was the only one to get home dry.

Prayer is our opportunity to come humbly before God with our praise, worship, and thanksgiving, and to lay our needs before Him and accept in faith whatever it seems to Him to be best to deal with those needs.

One example of this approach is found in the early church. Luke records in Acts 4 that the apostles were under threat from the authorities. Their response was to turn to prayer, but the structure of their prayer is significant. The prayer occupies about seven verses in the Bible, five of which praise God for His greatness and only two—the last two— addressing the apostles' problem. Even then there is no request for God to remove the threat or punish the authorities. Rather, the apostles sought boldness to cope with the threats. God answered by shaking the building in which they were gathered, thus demonstrating that He had heard them and also reminding them of His power.

Paul was a great believer in prayer. He had a problem and repeatedly prayed for its removal. God's answer was that his problem had been given to him so that God's power could be demonstrated through it.

> A thorn was given me in the flesh, a messenger of Satan to harass me, to keep me from becoming conceited. Three times I pleaded with the Lord about this, that it should leave me. But he said to me, "My grace is sufficient for you, for my power is made perfect in weakness." (2 Corinthians 12:7–9)

Obviously, it is easier to pray for a specific person or situation when God spells it out to us. Job's friends had angered God, and God told Job to pray for them and to tell them that the prayer would be answered.

> After the Lord had spoken these words to Job, the Lord said to Eliphaz the Temanite: "My anger burns against you and against your two friends, for you have not spoken of me what is right, as my servant Job has. Now therefore take seven bulls and seven rams and go to my servant Job and offer up a burnt offering for yourselves. And my servant Job shall pray for you, for I will accept his prayer not to deal with you according to your folly. For you have not spoken of me what is right, as my servant Job has." So Eliphaz the Temanite and Bildad the Shuhite and Zophar the Naamathite went and did what the Lord had told them, and the Lord accepted Job's prayer. And the Lord restored the fortunes of Job, when he had prayed for his friends. And the Lord gave Job twice as much as he had before. (Job 42:7–10)

Not only did God accept Job's prayer and withhold His punishment on the friends, but also He blessed Job as a result of the prayer, even though—or, perhaps, because—Job had not prayed for himself.

We should also remember that we are praying to a God who is not bound by time. This means, as Isaiah confirms for us, that God may answer our prayers even before we pray them. Isaiah 65:24 reads, "Before they call I will answer; while they are yet speaking I will hear."

It is not always easy to find the words to express the thoughts of our hearts. This is when it is comforting to remind ourselves that we do not need words. God knows of our love and devotion to Him, and He knows everything that we need. We can leave the rest to the Holy Spirit.

> The Spirit helps us in our weakness. For we do not know what to pray for as we ought, but the Spirit himself

intercedes for us with groanings too deep for words. And he who searches hearts knows what is the mind of the Spirit, because the Spirit intercedes for the saints according to the will of God. (Romans 8:26–27)

Lord, teach us to pray. (Luke 11:1)

THE SOVEREIGNTY OF
GOD IN SALVATION

Suggested Background Reading: Genesis 6 and Revelation 4

The sovereignty of God is God's dominion over the whole universe that He has created, and His rule over all things so as to "secure the accomplishment of the divine purposes".

From Scripture:

> Our God is in the heavens;
> he does all that he pleases.
> Their idols are silver and gold,
> the work of human hands.
> They have mouths, but do not speak;
> eyes, but do not see.
> They have ears, but do not hear;
> noses, but do not smell.
> They have hands, but do not feel;
> feet, but do not walk;
> and they do not make a sound in their throat.
> Those who make them become like them;
> so do all who trust in them. (Psalm 115:3–8)

For his dominion is an everlasting dominion, and his kingdom endures from generation to generation; all the inhabitants of the earth are accounted as nothing, and he does according to his will among the host of heaven and among the inhabitants of the earth; and none can stay his hand or say to him, "What have you done?" (Daniel 4:34b–35)

Behold, he snatches away; who can turn him back? Who will say to him, "What are you doing?" (Job 9:12)

But who are you, O man, to answer back to God? Will what is moulded say to its moulder, "Why have you made me like this?" (Romans 9:20)

In him we have obtained an inheritance, having been predestined according to the purpose of him who works all things according to the counsel of his will. (Ephesians 1:11)

From *The Belgic Confession*, Article 13:

We believe that this good God, after he created all things, did not abandon them to chance or fortune but leads and governs them according to his holy will, in such a way that nothing happens in this world without his orderly arrangement.

... This doctrine gives us unspeakable comfort since it teaches us that nothing can happen to us by chance but only by the arrangement of our gracious heavenly Father. He watches over us with fatherly care, keeping all creatures under his control, so that not one of the hairs on our heads (for they are all numbered) nor even a little bird can fall to the ground without the will of our Father.

In this thought we rest, knowing that he holds in check the devils and all our enemies, who cannot hurt us without his permission and will.

For that reason we reject the damnable error of the Epicureans, who say that God involves himself in nothing and leaves everything to chance.

From *The Absolute Sovereignty of God* by Rev. D. H. Kuiper:

We tread on holy ground when we take up the tremendous truth of divine sovereignty, and we ought to be reminded that there are aspects to this truth that we cannot understand. Nevertheless, scripture clearly and carefully sets this truth forth! The sovereignty of God is the exercise of His supremacy. God is the high and lofty One; no one is greater than He, equal to him, or anywhere near to Him. And when this great God acts, when He goes about His divine business, then he does so in perfect freedom! Sovereignty implies authority, and authority is the right to rule. It is the right to do what one wishes, to decide what is good and evil, to impose one's will on others and demand conformance; authority is the right to reward obedience and to punish disobedience! In close connection with this, sovereignty is the freedom to do what one pleases without being answerable to anyone. No one may question God as to what He is doing! The scripture drives this lesson home hard in such passages as Daniel 4:35, "And all the inhabitants of the earth are reputed as nothing: and He doest according to His will in the army of heaven, and among the inhabitants of the earth, and none can stay His hand, or say to Him, What doest Thou?"; Job 9:12, "Behold, He taketh away, who can hinder Him? Who will say unto Him, 'What doest Thou?'; Romans 9:20, "Who art thou, O man, that repliest against God? shall the thing formed say to Him that formed it, Why hast Thou made me thus?"

(See also the parable of our Lord in Matthew 20:1–16—the labourers who received one denarius each, even though some had worked much longer than others.)

A philosopher may assume that if we have responsibilities, we must be able to fulfil all of them, but this argument cannot be applied to theological studies. Looking back to the discussion about predestination, we are reminded that the fallen human being is incapable of turning to God in repentance without the grace of God working in his or her heart.

Only one can be sovereign. There can never be two sovereign beings in the same realm. It is impossible for two beings to have absolute authority over each other and be perfectly free to do as they please.

There is One who is eternal, independent, and sovereignly free, and that is God!

No limits can be placed upon God's sovereignty. There are many who would make restrictions or exceptions to divine sovereignty. They are willing to admit to sovereignty in respect to weather and climate, sickness and health, and wars and other disasters, but they want to draw the line when it comes to humankind! They try to exclude human thoughts, words, deeds, and destinies from the sovereignty of God! But this would destroy God's sovereignty. We will show that there cannot be a single exception of any kind!

This is in line with the comment which Jesus made when talking about earthly possessions: "No one can serve two masters, for either he will hate the one and love the other, or he will be devoted to the one and despise the other. You cannot serve God and money" (Matthew 6:24).

God has not made us to be puppets or robots. It is as if He is laying the options before us. We either submit to His sovereign will or face the consequences. God has given us the ability to choose to follow His will and obey His commands and enjoy a wonderful relationship with

Him, or we can opt to deny His sovereignty and live a life heading for eternity without Him. There is one thing we can be very sure about, and that is that denying God's sovereignty does not make Him any less sovereign. It follows that we can never thwart God's plans or stop Him from carrying out His will on earth or in heaven.

In Numbers 22 we read of an event in the history of the children of Israel when they were confronting the Moabites. They had just had some notable military victories, and the Moabites were worried. Balak, the Moabite king, called Balaam to come to his aid by cursing God's people. God intervened by sending an angel and causing his donkey to speak to him. Then Balaam ended up blessing the Israelites.

This is a clear case of God having a direct influence on the actions of a man so that His plans were fulfilled. When an account of this was read to the people in Nehemiah's day, they reacted by doing what God had told them, without any force on God's part.

> On that day they read from the book of Moses in the hearing of the people. And in it was found written that no Ammonite or Moabite should ever enter the assembly of God, for they did not meet the people of Israel with bread and water, but hired Balaam against them to curse them— yet our God turned the curse into a blessing. As soon as the people heard the law, they separated from Israel all those of foreign descent. (Nehemiah 13:1–3)

One question that is sometimes asked is why God allowed sin into the world in the first place. God placed Adam and Eve in a garden—the Garden of Eden—which He had planted Himself.

> And the Lord God planted a garden in Eden, in the east, and there he put the man whom he had formed. And out of the ground the Lord God made to spring up every tree that is pleasant to the sight and good for food. The Tree of Life was in the midst of the garden, and the Tree of

the Knowledge of Good and Evil. ... And the Lord God commanded the man, saying, "You may surely eat of every tree of the garden, but of the Tree of the Knowledge of Good and Evil you shall not eat, for in the day that you eat of it you shall surely die." (Genesis 2:8–9, 16–17)

Question 31. Why did God give Adam and Eve the ability to disobey Him?

It is interesting that we are told of two particular trees in this garden, the Tree of Life and the Tree of Knowledge of Good and Evil. Arguing about whether these were literal trees or figurative ones is not relevant at this point.

It may be helpful to look at the sequence of events here.

Firstly, both trees were in the garden, but only one—the tree of knowledge of good and evil—was not permitted to be used for food. The Tree of Life was there, and apparently Adam and Eve were allowed to eat from it. We are not told if they did so or not, but it seems very unlikely that they did, or else the subsequent events would be difficult to understand.

The next step in our sequence is to see that they did eat of the forbidden fruit. At this stage they had the God-given choice to obey God or not. They chose not to obey. The human race has suffered from that decision ever since.

Following their eating of the forbidden fruit, God expelled Adam and Eve from the garden to prevent them from eating the fruit of the Tree of Life. He took steps to prevent their return to that tree:

> Then the Lord God said, "Behold, the man has become like one of us in knowing good and evil. Now, lest he reach out his hand and take also of the Tree of Life and eat, and live for ever"—therefore the Lord God sent him out from

the garden of Eden to work the ground from which he was
taken. He drove out the man, and at the east of the garden
of Eden he placed the cherubim and a flaming sword that
turned every way to guard the way to the Tree of Life.
(Genesis 3:22–24)

We see God exercising His sovereignty in two different ways here.
Firstly, He gave Adam and Eve a command but did not force them
to obey Him. Secondly, He made it impossible for them to eat of the
Tree of Life. They had no choice here. God's sovereign will was put
into action.

The question remains: Why did God give Adam and Eve the ability
to choose to disobey Him? He must have known what would happen.

Nowhere are we told the answer to this question, and since we do not
know the mind of God, we can only take an educated guess. Possibly
the most likely explanation is that God wanted to show His power
and glory in salvation and thus to demonstrate His sovereignty in
heaven and on earth.

When looking at God's sovereignty in law, we noted that there are
laws, such as the law of gravity, which we have no means of breaking
but which God can change for a particular purpose when He wants
to. Other laws—the commands of God—are usually there for us to
choose to obey or else face the consequences of our disobedience. It is
rare for God to force us to obey Him as He did in the case of Balaam,
but in any case, our disobedience will always have a serious effect on
our relationship with God.

Even though we can choose to disobey God, we can never thwart His
plans. He will always have a way of achieving His sovereign will. He
may even use our wrongs to do so. An example of this might be seen
by thinking of those whose evil took our Lord to the cross at Calvary.
God's plan of salvation for the redemption of His elect from bondage
to sin required that Jesus go to the cross, and for this to be effective

it needed somebody to nail Him there. The Roman soldiers who did that were not puppets without any conscious involvement in their own actions; they were following their instincts of cruelty and hatred, unaware that they were working on God's behalf.

There are, however, a few events recorded in scripture where God did intervene directly in the decision-making processes of people. We read in Exodus 4:21, where God is telling Moses what reaction to expect from Pharaoh, "I will harden his heart, so that he will not let the people go."

There are seventeen additional references in Exodus to Pharaoh's heart being hardened (chapters 7–14), and at least seven of these are quite specific when noting that this was an act of God. God also hardened the hearts of the Egyptian army so that they pursued the Israelites into the Red Sea and were destroyed.

> And I will harden the hearts of the Egyptians so that they shall go in after them, and I will get glory over Pharaoh and all his host, his chariots, and his horsemen. And the Egyptians shall know that I am the Lord, when I have gained glory over Pharaoh, his chariots, and his horsemen. (Exodus 14:17–18)

These verses also give us a clearly stated reason for why God did this: so He would be glorified.

We read something similar about Sihon, the king of Heshbon, in Deuteronomy 2:30. In Joshua 11 we are told of a number of cities who were enemies of the Israelites who would not make treaties with them because God had hardened their hearts. This was so that they would fight against the Israelites and be defeated.

From *Big Truths for Young Hearts* by Bruce Ware

God rules the world he has made ... by guiding and directing it to accomplish or bring about everything that he has planned for it. ... Paul writes, "In him [Christ] we have obtained an inheritance, having been predestined according to the purpose of him [the Father] who works all things according to the counsel of his will" (Ephesians 1:11). God has a plan for the world he has made. He didn't create the world and then leave it alone to run by itself. Rather, God created the world with a very complete plan for how the world would develop and what would be accomplished through it. ... We can be sure that all of God's purposes and plans will be brought to pass since the God who made the world also rules the world he has made.

One of the names of God which is used 235 times in the scripture is "the Lord of Hosts". This is sometimes translated as "the Lord of Armies" or "the Lord All-Powerful", and it reminds us of God's sovereign power. This can be transliterated from the Hebrew as YHVH Sabaoth, which is the personal name for God linked to the word *Sabaoth*. To the Jewish mind, these titles are very limiting in contrast to the true significance of this name.

The Messianic Bible Society, translators of *The Messianic Prophecy Bible*, give us an insight into the meaning of *Sabaoth*:

Sabaoth is the feminine form of the Hebrew word *tsaba*, which means army, war or warfare. In fact, the Israeli military calls itself Tzva Haganah Le'Yisrael (literally, Israel Defence Army).

Yet, *tsaba* is often used in the Hebrew scriptures not to refer to a military army but a "vast array" or "host" of resources available to the infinite and sovereign God of the universe.

The first time we see the word *tsaba* is in the completion of Creation.

"Thus the heavens and the earth were completed, and all their hosts [*seba'am*]" (Genesis 2:1).

Here and in other scriptures, the masculine form of *tsaba* refers to the entire universe and all of God's perfect creation on earth. He made it. He is sovereign Lord over all of it: lightning and wind, sun and moon, man and woman, animals and plants. Everything!

Now, imagine the result when we combine *tsaba* with the personal name of God, YHVH—we get a name that gives us a glimpse into how marvellously almighty and all-powerful He truly is.

We see how great is the God who sent His Son to Calvary for our salvation when we look at His majesty through His name and title: YHVH Sabaoth.

The first recorded use of this name for God is found in the account of Samuel's birth. Hannah, in great distress because she is childless, pleads with the God of greatness and supreme power to grant her a son:

> O Lord of hosts [YHVH Sabaoth], if you will indeed look on the affliction of your servant and remember me and not forget your servant, but will give to your servant a son, then I will give him to the Lord all the days of his life, ... for all along I have been speaking out of my great anxiety and vexation. (1 Samuel 1:11, 16)

At that time, being childless was humiliating, seen as a sign of being cursed.

Hannah turned to the Creator who established the universe and brought life into existence as the only One who could deal with her situation.

Hannah may, or may not, have been aware of the gods of the surrounding Gentile nations. Many of these gods had specific roles to play, including fertility gods for pregnancy. None of these would have been of any help to Hannah at all. She went to the one God who could—and would—listen to her prayer and who had the infinite resources needed to answer it. She needed neither an army nor a military victory but the Comforter who would remove her shame in the community because she was barren.

Hannah found that YHVH Sabaoth could meet her every need when her son Samuel was born.

Question 32. *Was Hannah being selfish when she asked for a son? Was she bargaining with God?*

We have previously thought of the sovereignty of God in warfare, where we see Him as a warrior God and as the commander of armies. In Hannah, we see that YHVH Sabaoth is an intimate God who is with us in the details of our human experience.

Therefore, to anyone who knows God, it is futile to try fighting against Him! Because of the futility of fighting against Him, the efforts of Goliath of the Philistine army were doomed to failure.

> And the Philistine said, "I defy the ranks [maarakah] of Israel this day. Give me a man, that we may fight together." ... Then David said to the Philistine, "You come to me with a sword and with a spear and with a javelin, but I come to you in the name of Lord of Hosts—YHVH Sabaoth—the God of the armies [maarakah] of Israel, whom you have defied." (Samuel 17:10, 45) (Messianic Prophecy Bible)

Goliath, expecting a military battle, openly defied the greatness of Israel's armies. David reminded him that the battle was in God's hands, thereby making Goliath's weapons useless. The will of God to defeat the giant Goliath was accomplished because David fought the battle in God's way.

As Joshua took over the leadership of the Israelites to lead them across the Jordan River and to take possession of the Promised Land, a man appeared to him.

> When Joshua was by Jericho, he lifted up his eyes and looked, and behold, a man was standing before him with his drawn sword in his hand. And Joshua went to him and said to him, "Are you for us, or for our adversaries?" And he said, "No; but I am the commander of the army of the Lord. Now I have come." And Joshua fell on his face to the earth and worshipped and said to him, "What does my lord say to his servant?" And the commander of the Lord's army said to Joshua, "Take off your sandals from your feet, for the place where you are standing is holy." And Joshua did so. (Joshua 5:13–15)

So, we now see that the Lord of Hosts not only is the omnipotent sovereign over the whole of Creation, but also is perfectly holy. Even the seraphim who surround His throne are in awe of His holiness.

Isaiah 6:3 reads, "Holy, holy, holy is YHVH Sabaoth; the whole earth is full of His glory." This holiness is unlike any king or military ruler on earth can ever expect to possess.

The holiness and sovereignty of God are bound inseparably together. For us, we cannot aspire to His sovereignty—we should not even try—but we are called to be holy. We read in 1 Peter 1:16, "Since it is written, 'You shall be holy, for I am holy.'" Peter is quoting words found in Leviticus 11:45, 19:2 and 20:7.

It is tempting to assess our holiness by comparing ourselves with those around us, but this means taking our eyes off our Lord. The only true measure of holiness is against God's perfect holiness. He is sitting on His throne in heaven as the true sovereign God, so we should live our lives according to what He considers to be good behaviour.

As we gaze into His presence in penitent humility, we have our guilt removed and our sin atoned for as we are ready to be commissioned for His service.

> And I said: "Woe is me! For I am lost; for I am a man of unclean lips, and I dwell in the midst of a people of unclean lips; for my eyes have seen the King, the Lord of hosts!" Then one of the seraphim flew to me, having in his hand a burning coal that he had taken with tongs from the altar. And he touched my mouth and said: "Behold, this has touched your lips; your guilt is taken away, and your sin atoned for." And I heard the voice of the Lord saying, "Whom shall I send, and who will go for us?" Then I said, "Here am I! Send me." (Isaiah 6:5–8)

This is the very heart of God's sovereignty in salvation.

The sovereign God is still looking for people who will humbly answer His call to do His work for the extension of His kingdom and the fulfilment of His eternal purposes.

How do *we* answer His call?

Will we answer like Moses? "But he said, 'Oh, my Lord, please send someone else'" (Exodus 4:13).

Will we answer like Hannah? She took her situation to God and trusted His sovereignty for the answer.

Will we answer like David? He trusted in God's authority over His enemies.

Will we answer like Joshua? He showed respect for God's holiness.

Will we answer like Jonah? He tried to run away from God and needed to be asked twice.

Will we answer like Isaiah? He bowed in submission before a holy God and was ready to go wherever God sent him.

Will we answer like Noah? He obeyed God by building a vast boat according to God's instructions where there was no water, and saved the human race.

Will we answer like Asaph? He understood God's sovereignty in salvation.

We read in Psalm 80:19, "Restore us, O YHVH Elohim Sabaoth (O Lord God Sabaoth)! Let your face shine, that we may be saved!"

In everything we've seen as we have been looking at the scriptures concerning our God and Creator, there must be one central lesson which surpasses all the others: God is supreme; God is sovereign; God is over all things; and God is in control of all things. Therefore, above all else, we must worship Him and delight in Him. As *The Westminster Shorter Catechism* states: "The chief end of man is to know God and to enjoy Him forever." The main purpose of our lives is to know God and to enjoy Him. Now we don't often think of knowing God primarily as enjoying Him, but the truth we've learned from scripture is that because God is supreme and sovereign and perfect, knowing Him is the most perfect and joyful thing we'll ever do.

If you think of all the people you know and the relationships you have with them, then you must certainly conclude that those friends and family members whose company you enjoy most are those whom you agree with most. If you are constantly arguing with somebody and having a generally poor relationship with them, you do not enjoy spending time with them. Human relationships are very important to us, and we can be very sensitive to how they work for us. If we can understand how to build harmonious human relationships, then we have an excellent picture of how our relationship with God should be working.

Here is one final illustration to finish this exploration of the Sovereignty of God. If we have reached the point of realising that we need to obey God and follow His directions, we need to be listening to His voice and looking for signs of His leading. However, this does not mean that we should sit back and wait for Him to guide us, any more than we should make our own plans and ask God to bless them.

Some years ago, I was on a boat on the Norfolk Broads. At one point there is a low bridge (Potter Higham) that a boat can only just pass under with virtually no spare room at all. We used the services of a pilot to take the boat under this bridge. He came aboard and took the boat some distance away from the bridge before turning towards it and accelerating to full speed. He then aimed for the tiny gap under the bridge. We shot through with the narrowest of margins on either side. One of the passengers asked the pilot why we had gone through at such speed. His answer was that when the boat is travelling fast, it is very sensitive to the slightest movement of the rudder. When moving slowly, the boat responds slowly to the rudder control. By the time the pilot had explained this, the boat was moored for him to leave, but before he did leave, he turned the rudder again.

This time the steering mechanism of the boat had no response at all because the boat was not moving.

Sometimes God waits for us to be moving so that He can steer us in the direction He wants us to take.

Let us all remember that God is sovereign, and let His sovereignty make a positive impact on our lives as we seek to do His will, not our own.

Let us also remember that this God, who is sovereign and supreme in all things, is the same God who has bought our salvation by the death of His Son at Calvary. Those of us who have come to Him in repentance, asked for His forgiveness, and yielded our lives to Him can know with absolute certainty that He has the power to forgive us and cleanse us.

> If we confess our sins, he is faithful and just to forgive us our sins and to cleanse us from all unrighteousness. (1 John 1:9)

Salvation for God's people is assured.

> Now may the God of peace who brought again from the dead our Lord Jesus, the great shepherd of the sheep, by the blood of the eternal covenant, equip you with everything good that you may do his will, working in us that which is pleasing in his sight, through Jesus Christ, to whom be glory for ever and ever. Amen. (Hebrews 13:20–21)

May God richly bless you.

APPENDIX

F ollowing are extracts from commentaries which relate to God's act of creation. These form useful background reading for chapter 5. Where no publication details are given, the extracts may be found on Bible Gateway (biblegateway.com).

Matthew Henry
(died 1714)
(*Matthew Henry's Commentary on the Whole Bible*, World Bible)

"That God divided the light from the darkness, so put them asunder as that they could never be joined together, or reconciled; for what fellowship has light with darkness?" 2 Cor. 6:14. And yet he divided time between them, the day for light and the night for darkness, in a constant and regular succession to each other. Though the darkness was now scattered by the light, yet it was not condemned to a perpetual banishment, but takes its turn with the light, and has its place, because it has its use; for, as the light of the morning befriends the business of the day, so the shadows of the evening befriend the repose of the night, and draw the curtains about us, that we may sleep the better. See Job 7:2. God has thus divided time between light and darkness, because he would daily remind us that this is a world of mixtures and changes. In heaven there is perfect and perpetual light, and no darkness at all; in hell, utter darkness, and no gleam of light. In that world between these two there is a great gulf fixed; but, in this world, they are counter-changed, and we pass daily from one to another, that we may learn to expect the like vicissitudes in the providence of God, peace and trouble, joy and sorrow, and may set the one over-against the other, accommodating ourselves to both as we do to the light and darkness, bidding both welcome, and making the best of both.

That God divided them from each other by distinguishing names: He called the light day, and the darkness he called night. He gave them names, as the Lord of both; for the day is his, the night also is his, Ps. 74:16. He is the Lord of time, and will be so, till day and night shall come to an end, and the stream of time be swallowed up in the ocean of eternity. Let us acknowledge God in the constant succession of day and night, and consecrate both to his honour, by working for him every day and resting in him every night, and meditating in his law, day and night.

R. Payne Smith
(in *An Old Testament Commentary for English Readers*,
Charles Ellicott
Ed., Cassell 1884)

The Creative Days. (Genesis 1:3–5)

'**And God said.**—Voice and sound there could be none, nor was there any person to whom God addressed this word of power. The phrase, then, is metaphorical, and means that God enacted for the universe a law; and ten times we find the command similarly given. The beauty and sublimity of the language here used has often been noticed: God makes no preparation, He employs no means, needs no secondary agency. He speaks, and it is done. His word alone contains all things necessary for the fulfilment of His will. So in the cognate languages the word *Emir*, ruler, is literally, *speaker*. The Supreme One speaks: with the rest, to hear is to obey. God, then, by speaking, gives to nature a universal and enduring law. His commands are not temporary, but eternal; and whatever secondary causes were called into existence when the Elohim, by a word, created light, those same causes produce it now, and will produce it until God recalls His word. We have, then, here nature's first universal law. What is it?

Let there be light: and there was light.—The sublimity of the original is lost in our language by the cumbrous multiplication of particles. The Hebrew is *Yhi or wayhi or.* Light is not itself a substance, but is a condition or state of matter; and this primaeval light was probably electric, arising from the condensation and friction of the elements as they began to arrange themselves in order. And this, again, was due to what is commonly called the law of gravitation, or of the attraction of matter. If on the first day electricity and magnetism were generated, and the laws given which create and control them, we have in them the two most powerful and active energies of the present and of all time--or possibly two forms of one and the same busy and restless force. And the law thus given was that of gravitation, of which light was the immediate result.

(4) And God saw—This contemplation indicates, first, lapse of time; and next, that the judgement pronounced was the verdict of the Divine reason.

That it was good.—As light was a necessary result of motion in the world-mass, so was it indispensable for all that was to follow, inasmuch as neither vegetable nor animal life can exist without it. But the repeated approval by the Deity of each part and portion of this material universe (comp Ps civ. 31) also condemns all Manichaean theories, and asserts that this world is a noble home for man, and life a blessing, in spite of its solemn responsibilities.

And God divided ... The first three creative days are all days of order and distribution, and have been called "the three separations." But while on the first two days no new thing was created, but only the chaotic matter (described in verse" 2) arranged, on day three there was the introduction of vegetable life. The division on the first day, does not imply that darkness has a separate and independent existence, but that there were now periods of light and darkness; and thus, by the end of the first day our earth must have advanced far on its way towards its present state. (See Note, verse 5.) It is, however, even more probable that the ultimate results of each creative word are summed up in the account given of it. No sooner did motion begin, than the separation of the air and water from the denser particles must have begun too. The immediate result was light; removed by a greater interval was the formation of an open space round the contracting earth-ball; still more remote was the formation of continents and oceans; but the separations must have commenced immediately that the "wind of Elohim" began to brood upon and move the chaotic mass. How far these separations had advanced before there were recurrent periods of light and darkness is outside the scope of the Divine narrative, which is not geological, but religious.

(5) **God called the light Day ... Night.**—Before this distinction of night and day was possible there must have been outside the earth, not as yet the sun, but a bright phosphorescent mass, such as now enwraps that luminary; and secondly, the earth must have begun to revolve upon its axis. Consequent upon this would be not merely alternate periods of light and darkness, but also of heat and cold, from which would result important effects upon the formation of the earth's crust. Moreover, in thus giving "day" and "night" names, God ordained language, and that vocal sounds should be the symbols of things. This, law already looks forward to the existence of man, the one being on earth who calls things by their names.

And the evening and the morning.—Literally, *And was an evening and was a morning day one,* the definite article not being used till verse 31, when we have "day the sixth," which was also the last of the creative days.

The word "evening" means a mixture. It is no longer the opaque darkness of a world without light, but the intermingling of light and darkness, (comp. Zech. xiv. 6, 7). This is followed by a "morning," that is, a *breaking forth* of light. Evening is placed first because there was a progress from a less to a greater brightness and order and beauty. The Jewish method of calculating, the day from sunset to sunset was not the cause, but the result of this arrangement.

The First Day.—A creative day is not a period of twenty-four hours, but an *aeon*, or period of indefinite duration, as the Bible itself teaches us. For in chap. ii. 4 the six days of this narrative are described as and summed up in one day, creation being there regarded, not in its successive stages, but as a whole. So, by the common consent of commentators, the seventh day, or day of God's rest, is that age in which we are now living, and which will continue until the consummation of all things. So, in. Zech. xiv. 7 the whole Gospel dispensation is called "one day;" and constantly in Hebrew, as probably in all languages, *day* is used in a very indefinite manner, as, for instance, in Deut. ix.1. Those, however; who adopt the very probable suggestion of Kurtz, that the revelation of the manner of creation was made in a succession of representations or pictures displayed before the mental vision of the tranced seer, have no difficulties. He saw the dark gloom of evening pierced by the bright morning light: that was day one. Again, an evening cleft by the light, and he saw air opening space -expanding itself around the world: that was day two. Again, darkness and light, and on the surface of the earth he saw the waters rushing down into the seas: that was day three. And so-on. What else could he call these periods but days? But as St. Augustine pointed out, there was no sun then, and "it is very difficult for us to imagine what sort of days these could be" (De Civ. Dei, xi 6,7). It must further be observed that this knowledge of the stages of creation could only have been given by revelation, and that the agreement of the Mosaic record with geology is so striking that there is no real difficulty in believing it to be inspired. The difficulties arise almost entirely, from popular fallacies or the mistaken views of commentators. Geology has done noble service for religion in sweeping away the mean views of God's method of working which used formerly to prevail. We may add that among the Chaldeans a cosmic day was a period of 43,200 years, being the equivalent of the cycle of the procession of the equinoxes (Lenormant, Les Origines de l'Histoire, p. 233).

The New Bible Commentary
(IVF 1953)

What was the "day". which marked the divine stages of the work of creation? It is contended by some that this is an ordinary day of twenty-four hours. In support of this it is pointed out that the periods of evening and morning are specifically mentioned, but there are serious difficulties in the way of accepting this interpretation. Others conceive of these days as days of dramatic vision, the story being presented to Moses in a series of revelations spread over six days. This is an intensely interesting suggestion, but can scarcely be regarded as more than a conjecture. A third view is held by many at the present time. This is that each "day" represents, not a period of twenty-four hours, but a geological age. It is pointed out that the sun, the measurer of planetary time, did not exist during the first three days; further, that the term "day" is used in ii. 4 for the whole sixfold period of creation; and that in other parts of Scripture the word "day" is employed figuratively of a time of undefined length, as in Ps. xc. 4. The chief difficulty attaching to this last interpretation is the mention of "evening and "morning", but this may perhaps be but a purely figurative way of saying that the creation was characterized by clearly defined epochs.

The amount of creation is given with a spiritual and religious aim. An account of the origin of things is provided here without which the relation between God and man would be left undefined. The revelation is put forward for the faith of the true worshipper. "Through faith we understand that the worlds were formed by the word of God, so that things which are seen were not made of things which do appear" (Heb. xi. 3). The reader of this chapter who has a personal experience of God in Christ can readily believe the record it contains; but the things it describes are so astounding, and so beyond the range of scientific verification, that it is not surprising that some find great difficulty here. A second purpose in this narrative is to place man at the climax of earthly creation. Stage by stage the work of God proceeds until man is reached as the crown of all.

Warren Wiersbe

In verse 4, God deemed the light "good." In Scripture, light is associated with Christ (8:12), the Word of God (Ps. 119:105,130), God's people (Matt. 5:14–16; Eph. 5:8), and God's blessing (Prov. 4:18), while darkness is associated with Satan (Eph. 6:12), sin (Matt. 6:22– 23; John 3:19–21), death (Job 3:4–6, 9), spiritual ignorance (John 1:5), and divine judgement (Matt. 8:12). This explains why God separated the light from the darkness, for the two have nothing in common. God's people are to "walk in the light" (1 John 1:5–10), for "what communion hath light with darkness?" (2 Cor. 6:14–16; see Eph. 5:1–14).

From the very first day of creation, God established the principle of separation. Not only did He separate the light from the darkness (Gen. 1:4) and the day from the night (v. 14), but later He also separated the waters above from the waters beneath (vv. 6–8), and the land from the waters (vv. 9–10). Through Moses, God commanded the people of Israel to remain separated from the nations around them (Ex. 34:10–17; Deut. 7:1–11), and when they violated this commandment, they suffered. God's people today need to be careful in their walk (Ps. 1:1) and not be defiled by the world (Rom. 12:1–2; James 1:6-8; 4:4; 1 John 2:15-17).

Since God is the Creator, He has the right to call things whatever He pleases, and thus we have "day" and "night." The word "day" can refer to the portion of time when the sun is visible as well as to the whole period of twenty-four hours composed of "evening and morning" (Gen. 1:5). Sometimes biblical writers used "day" to describe a longer period of time in which God accomplishes some special purpose, such as "the day of the Lord" (Isa 2:12) or "the day of judgement" (Matt. 10:15).

When we speak about spiritual things, it's important that we use God's dictionary as well as His vocabulary. Words carry meanings and giving the wrong meaning to a word could lead to serious trouble. It would be fatal to a patient if a physician confused "arsenic" with "aspirin," so medical people are very careful to use accurate terminology. The "Christian vocabulary" is even more important because eternal death could be the consequence of confusion. The Bible explains and illustrates words like sin, grace, forgiveness, justification, and faith, and to change their meanings is to replace God's truth with lies. "Woe unto them that call evil good, and good evil; that put darkness for light, and light for darkness; that put bitter for sweet, and sweet for bitter" (Isa. 5:20).

Asbury Bible Commentary
(Zondervan 1992)

1. The origin of the universe (1:1-2:3)
God occupies centre stage in this chapter. Thirty-four times, in as many verses, the word God is paired with an action verb. The writer is more concerned with the "who" of creation than with the process or "how" of creation. The brevity of the chapter further underscores the scant regard the author demonstrates in the process of creation per se. Sun, moon, sky, and sea are summarily dismissed in a few brief sentences despite modern human fascination with the creative process. As such, the primary purpose of the narrative is to elicit praise of the Creator. In that sense, ch.1 must be considered a liturgical hymn.

The idea of a liturgical hymn is enhanced by the symmetrical form of the chapter. Each new creation event is announced by the formula and God said, "Let there be" or something similar. Each creation is confirmed (and it was so or "God made/created/did it"). Each time but one the creation period is validated: And God saw that it was good. Finally, each Creation period is concluded with the words: And there was evening and there was morning. The structure of ch.1 implies a creedal confession in the God who creates rather than a scientific dissertation about the origin of the world. The Bible is mute regarding the various scientific theories on how the world came into being, apart from affirming God's sovereign, creative role in it.

NIV Application Commentary

God created. The text next speaks of God's activity using the Hebrew word *bara'*, unanimously rendered "created." Again, however, we must be careful to remember that to interpret the Bible accurately, we must understand bara' in Hebrew terms. The verb occurs forty- eight times in the Old Testament and has some curious features worth noting.

(1) It takes only God as its subject and therefore must be identified as a characteristically divine activity.

(2) The objects of this verb are widely varied. They include people groups (Ps. 102:18; Ezek. 21:30); Jerusalem (Isa. 65:18); phenomena such as wind, fire, cloud, destruction, calamity, or darkness (Ex. 34:10; Num 16:30; Isa. 45:7; Amos 4:13); and abstractions such as righteousness, purity, or praise (Ps. 51:10;Isa. 57:19). Even when the object is something that could be "manufactured" ("creatures of the sea" in Gen. 1:21), the point need not necessarily be physical manufacturing as much as assigning roles. This direction is picked up nicely in Genesis 5:2, where God "creates" people male and female, that is, with established gender functions. In all of these cases, something is brought into existence, but rarely does the statement concern the issue of physical matter.

Indeed, *bara'* never occurs in a context in which materials are mentioned. Instead of suggesting manufacture of matter out of nothing, its usages suggest that manufacture is not the issue. The essence of bara' concerns bringing heaven and earth into existence and focuses on operation through organization and assignment of roles and functions. Even in English we use the verb "create" within a broad range of contexts but rarely apply it to material things (i.e., parallel in concept to "manufacture"). One can create a piece of art, but that expression does not suggest manufacture of the canvas or paint. Even more abstractly, one can create a situation (e.g., havoc) or a condition (an atmosphere). In these cases, the verb indicates the establishment of a role or function. When someone creates a department, a curriculum, or an advertising campaign, it is an organizational task. One puts it together and makes it work. Hebrew usage of *bara'* is similar. Perhaps an English verb that captures this idea less ambiguously is "to design" (though bara' includes both planning and implementing the design).

When we are doing exegesis, we are not asking the question, "What does my belief system affirm that God has done?" nor even, "What would Israel's belief system affirm God was responsible for?" Rather, we must ask, "What is the text asserting that God did in this context?" The above analysis suggests that in the seven-day initial period God brought the cosmos into operation (which defines existence) by assigning roles and functions. Later Scripture supports our belief that God also made all of the matter of which the cosmos is composed (and that he made it out of nothing, Col. 1:16–17; Heb. 11:3), but that is not what Genesis means by the use of bara'. The origin of matter is what our society has taught us is important (indeed, that matter is all there is), but we cannot afford to be so distracted by our cultural ideas. The existence of matter was not the concern of the author of Genesis.

Encyclopaedia of the Bible

Day The Bible includes a number of different uses of the word.

1. It often refers to the hours of daylight between dawn and dusk (Gen 1:5; 8:22; Acts 20:31; etc.). In OT times this was divided into morning, noon, and evening (Ps 55:17), or the time of the day might be indicated by the use of such expressions as sunrise, heat of the day, cool of the day, sunset, and the like. The Babylonians reckoned their days from sunrise to sunrise; the Romans, from midnight to midnight; the Greeks and the Jews, from sunset to sunset. The first mention in the Bible of a twelve-hour day is found in John 11:9. The division of the day into twelve-hour periods came from the Babylonians.
2. The concept of a legal or civil day, the period between two successive sun risings, goes back to the creation story (Gen 1:14, 19) and is found throughout the Bible (Luke 9:37; Acts

21:26). The only day of the week to which the Jews gave a name was the Sabbath; they used ordinal numbers for the days, although the day before the Sabbath was often called the day of Preparation (Matt 27:62); Mark 15:42; Luke 23:54; John 19:31,42). The night was subdivided into watches—first, middle, and morning. The Romans had four watches. Acts 23:23 shows that the night also was divided into twelve hours.

3. The word often is used in the sense of an indefinite period of time: the whole creative period (Gen 2:4), day of God's wrath (Job 20:28), day of trouble (Ps 20:1), day of the Lord of hosts (Isa 2:12), day of salvation (2 Cor 6:2) day of Jesus Christ (Phil 1:6). The pl. is sometimes used in the sense of "time of," as in the "days of Abraham" (Gen 26:18), the "days of Noah" (Matt 24:37), or of the span of human life, as in "the days of Adam… were eight hundred years" (Gen 5:4), "I will lengthen your days" (1 Kings 3:14). The eternal God is called "the Ancient of Days" (Dan 7:9, 13).

4. Many times the word is used fig. When Jesus said, "We must work the works of him who sent me, while it is day; night comes, when no one can work" (John 9:4), "day" means the time of opportunity for service. Jesus said that because His disciples saw "the light of this world" as they walked "in the day" (John 11:9), and He Himself claimed to be "the light of the world" (John 8:12). Paul called Christians "sons of light and sons of the day," contrasting them with those who were "of the night or of darkness" (1 Thess 5:5). When Paul wrote, "the night is far gone, the day is at hand" (Rom 13:12), he meant by "day" the time of eschatological salvation. There will be perpetual day in the final state of perfection (Rev 21:25).

5. There are special days set aside for and belonging in a peculiar sense to Jehovah, such as the Sabbath day (Gen 2:3; Exod 20:8–11), the Passover (Exod 12:14), and the Day of Atonement (Lev 16:29–31). On these days no labour was to be done and special rituals were observed.

6. In both Testaments is frequent mention of "the day of the Lord" and similar terms used to designate it. This is not a

particular day, but a period of time at the end of history when God will bring judgment upon godless peoples and vindicate His name (Isa 2:12;13:9; Ezek 7:7, 8; Matt 24; 25; 2 Thess 2:1–12). After this supernatural intervention of God in history, He will set up His eternal kingdom (Rev 20–22), and all things will be consummated in Christ (Eph_1:10).

7. The phrase, "the last days," seems to include in its broadest meaning the whole period from the Cross to the Second Advent (Acts 2:17; 2 Tim 3:1; Heb 1:2; 2 Peter 3:3,_4).

Reformation Study Bible (Ligonier Ministries)

God shows He is ruler of the cosmos by naming its spheres (17:5; cf. Num. 32:38; 2 Kin 23:24; 24:17). By His creative commands and designations, God gave existence and meaning to everything according to His eternal counsel. For God Himself there are no mysteries, and all creation has coherence and meaning within His will. For man, the beginning of wisdom is the fear of the all-wise God (Prov. 1:7).

First Day. This presentation of the creation week enables God's covenant people to imitate the Creator in their weekly pattern of work and rest (Ex. 20:11; 31:13,_17).

Reformed scholars have proposed several interpretations of the creative "day." Some view these as literal, sequential, 24-hour days. This interpretation usually entails the view that the earth is relatively "young" (c. 10,000 years old or less). Other scholars, noting that the Hebrew word for "day" (*yom*) can refer to periods of time (e.g., 2:4), have proposed the "day-age theory," that the creative "days" refer to extended ages or epochs of time. Still others suggest that literal, 24-hour days are intended, but that these days were separated by extended periods of time. Finally, some scholars argue that the "days" of creation constitute a literary framework (vv. 3–31 note) designed to teach that God alone is the creator of an orderly universe, and to call upon human beings made in the image of the creator God to reflect God's creative activity in their own pattern of labour (2:2; Ex._31:17).

This "framework hypothesis" views the days of creation as God's gracious accommodation to the limitations of human knowledge— an expression of the infinite Creator's work in terms understandable to finite and frail human beings. This last group of scholars observes that the universe gives the appearance of great antiquity, that the phrase "morning and evening" seems inconsistent with the "day-age" theory, and that the notion of intervening ages between isolated 24- hour days is not apparent from the text.

Wayne Grudem
(Systematic Theology: An Introduction to Biblical Doctrine, IVP, 1994)*

What shall we conclude about the length of days in Genesis 1? It does not seem at all easy to decide with the information we now have. It is not simply a question of "believing the Bible" or "not believing the Bible," nor is it a question of "giving in to modern science" or "rejecting the clear conclusions of modern science". Even for those who believe in the complete truthfulness of Scripture (such as the present author), and who retain some doubt about the exceptionally long periods of time scientists propose for the age of the earth (such as the present author), the question does not seem to be easy to decide. At present, considerations of the power of God's creative word and the immediacy with which it seems to bring response, the fact that "evening and morning" and the numbering of days still suggest twenty-four-hour days, and the fact that God would seem to have no purpose for delaying the creation of man for thousands or even millions of years, seem to me to be strong considerations in favour of the twenty-four-hour day position. But even here there are good arguments on the other side: To the one who lives forever, for whom one day is as a thousand years, and a thousand years as one day" (2 Peter 3:8), who delights in gradually working out all his purposes over time, perhaps 15 billion years is just the right amount of time to take in preparing the universe for man's arrival and 4.5 billion years in preparing the earth. The evidence of incredible antiquity in the universe would then serve as a vivid reminder of the even more amazing nature of God's eternity, just as the incredible size of the universe causes us to wonder at God's even greater omnipresence and omnipotence.

Therefore, with respect to the length of days in Genesis 1, the possibility must be left open that God has chosen not to give us enough information to come to a clear decision on this question, and the real test of faithfulness to Him may be the degree to which we can act charitably toward those who in good conscience and full belief in God's Word hold a different position on this matter.

Both "Old Earth" and "Young Earth" theories are valid options for Christians who believe the Bible today.